Chocol

Chocolate

OVER 250 RECIPES FOR CAKES, COOKIES, DESSERTS, PARTY FOOD, AND DRINKS

THUNDER BAY
P · R · E · S · S

San Diego, California

Thunder Bay Press
An imprint of the Advantage Publishers Group
5880 Oberlin Drive, San Diego, CA 92121-4794
www.thunderbaybooks.com

All notations of errors or omissions should be addressed to
Thunder Bay Press, Editorial Department, at the above address. All other correspondence
(author inquiries, permissions) concerning the content of this book should be addressed to
Salamander Books Ltd, 8 Blenheim Court, Brewery Road, London, N7 9NY, U.K.

ISBN 1-57145-956-1
Library of Congress Cataloging-in-Publication Data available upon request.

Printed in China
1 2 3 4 5 07 06 05 04 03

Credits

EDITOR: Katherine Edelston
DESIGNER: Cara Hamilton
PRODUCTION: Don Campaniello
COLOR REPRODUCTION: Anorax Imaging Ltd
PRINTED AND BOUND BY: Sino Publishing House Ltd, China

Contents

8
Introduction

46
Hot
Desserts

84
Frozen
Desserts

140
Cold
Desserts

220
Cakes

280
Pastries

326
Cookies &
Bars

362
Sweets &
Drinks

396
Index

Introduction

Chocolate has been valued and enjoyed all over the world for centuries, but the chocolate we know today bears little resemblance to that consumed in such great quantities by the Aztec emperor Montezuma in the sixteenth century. There are few people who can resist a chocolate cake or dessert, and for some it is almost an addiction. This is hardly surprising, for chocolate contains a natural amphetamine that stimulates the central nervous system to produce a feeling of well-being.

Choosing the right chocolate for a particular recipe can be confusing. In this book, you'll find descriptions of the different types of chocolate available, with instructions for melting and molding chocolate successfully, plus ideas for making all kinds of chocolate decorations.

A collection of recipes—guaranteed to delight all chocolate lovers—completes the book. There are variations of traditional favorites, as well as many new and interesting ideas for mouthwatering desserts, tempting cakes and pastries, sweets, and beverages. From elaborate concoctions to some very simple ideas, there are recipes for every occasion. Many can be prepared in advance and quite a few require no cooking at all.

The History of Chocolate

The cacao or cocoa tree is native to South America, where it has been cultivated since the seventh century by many people, including the Aztecs, Mayans, and Incas. They brewed a drink from cocoa beans and valued the beans so highly that they were also used as currency.

The first Europeans to see the cocoa bean were those on Columbus's fourth voyage in 1502. He returned to Spain with a collection of treasures from the New World, among which were some dark brown beans, but no one knew what to do with them. It wasn't until twenty years later, when the Spanish conquistador Hernando Cortez arrived in Mexico, that the pleasures of the cocoa bean were discovered.

Cortez found the emperor of the Aztecs, Montezuma, consuming up to fifty cups a day of a bitter, pungent drink, called *cacahuatl* or *xocoatl*, from a golden goblet. The drink was believed to be an aphrodisiac, and the beans from which it was brewed a gift from the gods. The enterprising Cortez took some cocoa beans with him when he returned to Spain (this time taking the method of preparing them, too). On the trip home, he planted some of the beans in Africa.

The Spanish king and his court were enchanted by this new dark, rich drink and, having sweetened it with sugar and flavored it with vanilla and cinnamon, they jealously guarded the secrets of its delights for over a hundred years.

In 1606, the secret leaked out when Antonio Carletti took the recipe to Italy. From that point on, the pleasures of drinking chocolate spread quickly across Europe.

At the beginning of the seventeenth century, the exotic new chocolate drink was an expensive luxury greatly appreciated only by the aristocrats at many European courts, but soon chocolate houses were springing up all over Europe as meeting places for the fashionable and learned. White's and The Cocoa Tree were the most popular chocolate houses in London, frequented by Samuel Pepys and many poets, playwrights, and would-be politicians.

The chocolate drink that enjoyed such popularity then was made from a crumbly, coarse paste that had a high fat content. Two centuries later, in 1828, a Dutchman named Van Houten invented a press to extract the fat or cocoa butter from the beans, leaving behind a powder that could be dissolved in water to make a chocolate drink. Later, in 1847, the English firm Fry & Sons added sugar and chocolate liquor to the cocoa butter to produce the first eating chocolate.

In the early days all eating chocolate was plain, with a rough, grainy texture. The first milk chocolate was made in Switzerland in 1876, and the Swiss continued to improve their recipe until it became the smooth-melting chocolate we know today.

Since then, our appetite for chocolate has continued to increase, with eating chocolate having long ago overtaken drinking chocolate in popularity.

Producing Chocolate

The cacoa tree (*Theobroma cacao*) is only cultivated in the tropical zone within twenty degrees of the equator. West Africa produces 60 percent of the world's supply of cocoa, while Brazil is the largest producer in South America. The trees start producing pods when they are three to five years old. They bloom throughout the year but only twenty to thirty of the 10,000 blossoms produced by each tree develop into fully grown, spindle-shaped fruits or pods. These form on the trunk and thickest branches of the tree. Each one contains thirty to forty white or purple seeds—the cocoa beans.

After harvesting, the pods are slit open and the beans and pulp scooped out and piled into heaps on banana or plantain leaves. They are covered with a layer of leaves and left to ferment for five to six days. As the temperature in the heap rises, the pulp becomes liquid and drains away. During this process the beans turn dark brown, the shells become thinner, and the cocoa flavor really develops.

After fermentation, the beans are left to dry in the sun, then shipped to manufacturers for processing.

The first processing stage is roasting, which

further develops the cocoa flavor. After roasting, the kernels or nibs are extracted from the beans and ground. The friction of grinding extracts the cocoa butter, leaving a thick paste called chocolate liquor. When cooled, this hardens to form unsweetened cooking chocolate. Further pressing of the nibs extracts even more cocoa butter, and the remaining solid cake is ground to form cocoa powder.

To make semisweet eating chocolate, extra cocoa butter and sugar are added to the chocolate liquor. To make milk chocolate, milk, in a dried form, is also added.

The next stage is called conching, in which the semiliquid mixture is poured into machines that grind, mix, and slightly heat the ingredients for several days. This evaporates moisture, improves the texture, and develops the flavor.

Before chocolate is molded in bars or used for coating purposes, it is tempered by cooling very carefully to 79°F (26°C). This further improves the texture, gloss, and keeping qualities of chocolate.

Types of Chocolate

Baking chocolate is unsweetened chocolate for cooking. It is excellent used in baked goods.

Semisweet chocolate is the most useful type for cooking, as it gives a good, strong flavor. However, quality varies considerably according to the proportion of cocoa solids listed in the ingredients. The higher the percentage of cocoa solids, the better the chocolate. It should contain a minimum of 34 percent—the best chocolate contains 50 percent or more.

Milk chocolate is not satisfactory for use in cooking, but if melted it may be piped onto semisweet chocolate for a decorative effect. It may also be used for molding Easter eggs for children, who often prefer the flavor of milk chocolate.

White chocolate is not really chocolate at all, as it comprises cocoa butter, milk, and sugar, but contains no chocolate liquor. It is not usually used for cooking because it lacks flavor, but its creamy texture makes it suitable for use in cold desserts. It gives an interesting contrast when combined with semisweet chocolate.

Couverture is generally only available to professional confectioners. It has a high cocoa butter content and flows very smoothly, making it ideal for coating purposes. It must be tempered before use.

Compound or confectionery coatings contain vegetable oil instead of added cocoa butter, which makes them considerably cheaper than true chocolate. For most purposes, the flavor and texture are inferior and this type of chocolate is not recommended for use in this collection of recipes.

Unsweetened cocoa powder is a convenient and inexpensive way of achieving a strong chocolate flavor in baking, but it is not suitable for use in uncooked dishes. A good substitute for bitter chocolate is a mixture of three tablespoons unsweetened cocoa powder and one tablespoon butter. Add one tablespoon of sugar to provide a substitute for semisweet chocolate.

Sweetened chocolate powder is a mixture of unsweetened cocoa powder and sugar. It is too sweet for use in cooking unless the sugar in the recipe is reduced accordingly.

Storing Chocolate

Semisweet and milk chocolate have a shelf life of about one year, but white chocolate tends to deteriorate after about eight months. The shelf life is, of course, dependent upon the chocolate being stored in the correct conditions. It should be well wrapped and stored in a cool place, but not in the refrigerator. Chocolate stored at below 55°F (13°C) will usually develop a bloom and putrify when transferred to room temperature. When chocolate is stored above 70°F (21°C), it will also develop a bloom.

Bloom is a grayish-white coating that appears on the surface of chocolate. It affects the appearance but does not impair the flavor, nor is it an indication that the chocolate has deteriorated. Fat bloom is caused by heating and cooling chocolate; it is greasy and easily rubbed off. Sugar bloom shows up as a white crust of sugar crystals on chocolate that has been stored in a refrigerator; it cannot be removed.

Carob

Although processed carob and chocolate look similar, they are not related in any way. Carob is not chocolate at all—it is a member of the legume family.

Grown all over the Mediterranean and in the United States, carob trees can take up to sixty-five years to produce fruit regularly. The flowers develop into pods that eventually develop into dark brown, leathery pods with a glossy surface. The pod is roasted, milled, and sieved to produce carob powder, in which form it is ready for use in cooking, and is made into bars by mixing with sugar, vegetable fats, skimmed milk powder, lecithin, and flavoring.

It has been popular with health food enthusiasts for some years, as it is rich in vitamins and minerals, contains no refined sugar, theobromine, caffeine, or oxalic acid, and contains fewer calories than chocolate.

It can be substituted for chocolate in many recipes, although when melted it will not have the shiny finish of chocolate. When used in cooking, it has a mild chocolate flavor and pale color. However, for the chocolate lover and connoisseur, there is no substitute for the real thing.

Melting Chocolate

Great care must be taken when melting chocolate, as it scorches very easily if overheated and will develop into hard, grainy lumps. This will also happen if any liquid or steam comes into contact with the chocolate while it is melting.

Chocolate can be safely melted with a small amount of liquid if they are put into the bowl together. It will melt more evenly and quickly if it is broken, chopped, or cut in small, even pieces. Do not stir the chocolate until it has melted, and even then stir it very gently. If by mischance the chocolate does develop hard, grainy lumps, it can sometimes be restored by adding a little vegetable oil.

Chocolate can also be added to a large quantity of hot liquid and left to melt, without stirring. Stir when completely melted to make a very smooth mixture.

White chocolate is particularly sensitive to heat; therefore, extra care is needed when melting. When using the microwave method, set the oven on 50 percent power and cook in one- to two-minute bursts, stirring the chocolate at each interval.

The following are the most successful ways of melting chocolate.

Over hot water: Place chocolate in a bowl set over a saucepan of simmering water; the bottom of the bowl must not touch the water. Remove pan from heat and let stand until chocolate has melted.

In an oven: Place chocolate in a shallow dish in a 225°F (110°C) oven. Leave until chocolate is soft.

In a plastic bag: This is a convenient way of melting a small quantity of chocolate, particularly if it is required for piped decoration. Place chocolate in a heavy-gauge plastic bag, seal, and set the bag in hot, but not boiling, water. When chocolate has melted, cut a corner of the bag and use chocolate as required.

In a microwave: This is a very convenient way to melt chocolate. Place chocolate in a microwave-safe bowl and heat for about 2 minutes on full power, stirring occasionally. The exact time depends on the quantity of chocolate, size of bowl, and wattage of oven.

Using melted chocolate

Allow melted chocolate to cool slightly. Stir and then combine with other ingredients.

Small quantities of butter or oil may be added after melting to make the chocolate smoother and more fluid, if desired, for icing and dipping.

Add chocolate to other liquid ingredients, rather than pouring other liquids into the chocolate.

When using melted chocolate in cake mixtures, add it after creaming the fat and sugar and before adding the eggs and flour.

For soufflé and mousse mixtures, combine the melted chocolate with the egg yolks and flavoring before adding the cream and egg whites.

Bought Decorations

A vast array of ready-made chocolate decorations are available for effortless finishes.

Pieces of semisweet or milk chocolate can be added whole to cakes and cookies—they retain their shape even when cooked—or used as cake decorations. Chocolate chips can also be melted and used like chocolate in cooking; they are convenient to use, as they melt easily.

Chocolate buttons, either plain or covered, are used for decorating children's cakes. They lend themselves to many ideas, such as tiles on a gingerbread roof.

Chocolate flakes, used whole, are an attractive decoration for cakes, drinks, and ice cream sundaes. Crumbled, it makes a convenient alternative to grated chocolate. Mini flakes are also available at some stores.

Chocolate vermicelli (sprinkles) are available in milk and semisweet chocolate. They are extremely convenient for coating the tops and sides of cakes, and for sprinkling over ice cream. They are also used for coating chocolate truffles. The kind most usually found in shops is really chocolate-coated sugar strands—real chocolate vermicelli is hard to find.

Chocolate cups and shells are available in a variety of shapes and sizes. Larger ones may be filled with cream and fruit, mousse mixtures, or ice cream, while small cups are suitable for filling with liqueur-flavored truffle mixture to serve with coffee at the end of a meal.

Other chocolate decorations can be found in a wide variety of shapes. In addition to those sold specifically as decorations, there are many chocolates to be found on the confectionery counter that are ideal for giving a decorative finishing touch to cakes, desserts, and ice creams. Thin after-dinner mints look attractive arranged around the sides of cakes, or they may be cut in triangles and used to decorate a chocolate mousse.

Stick-shaped chocolates are available in a range of flavors, such as coffee, mint, and orange. As well as making excellent decorations for ice cream, they are delicious broken up and incorporated into the ice cream mixture. Thin chocolate wafers may be used as they are, cut in triangles, or crumbled over the top of a cake.

Chocolate pieces, after-dinner mints, flakes, and buttons

Chocolate dots, sprinkles, chocolate sticks, and chocolate leaves

Homemade Decorations

Homemade chocolate decorations give a professional finish to a variety of cakes, puddings, and desserts.

With a little practice, it is possible to produce an endless range of decorations, from the simple to the elaborate. Until you become more experienced and confident, experiment with compound coating, as it is easier to work with and any disasters can be remelted and used again. Leave decorations in a cool place to set, but do not put them in a refrigerator or they will develop an unattractive bloom.

Grated chocolate. This is one of the most effective and simple chocolate decorations. Different effects are achieved according to how coarsely the chocolate is grated.

Use grated chocolate to cover the top and/or sides of a cake that has been iced with whipped cream or butter cream. Roll truffles or sweets in finely grated chocolate to coat them.

Grated chocolate can also be sprinkled over a wide variety of desserts and ice cream for a simple finish. For an attractive cake or cheesecake topping, sprinkle alternate bands of grated chocolate and confectioners' sugar over the top, using strips of waxed paper as a guide.

Curls. Use a thick bar of chocolate and make sure it is neither too cold nor too warm. Scrape a vegetable peeler along one long edge of the chocolate bar and allow the curls to fall onto a plate. Lift them carefully onto the dessert to be decorated.

Caraque. Pour a thin layer of melted chocolate over a firm, flat surface, spreading quickly with a knife to smooth. Let stand until set, then, holding the blade of a knife at a 45-degree angle, push it along the surface of the chocolate to form long scrolls. As the curls form, lift them carefully with the point of a knife. If necessary, caraque may be kept in a box in the refrigerator for a short while until required.

Leaves. Any fresh leaves may be used—as long as they are not poisonous—but rose leaves are particularly suitable because they have prominent veins and are an attractive shape for decorating.

Wash and dry the leaves thoroughly, then brush the underside with melted chocolate or carefully dip into the chocolate. Place on waxed paper until completely set, then gently lift the tip of the leaf and peel it away from the paper.

Piped chocolate. Melted chocolate piped directly onto a cake or dessert is a very simple way of achieving a professional finish. It may be piped as writing or a definite pattern, but an even easier and just as effective technique is to drizzle a random pattern. Light chocolate piped over dark chocolate, or the two combined in a piped design, look particularly attractive.

To apply a feather design, cover the top of a large cake or individual ones with plain or coffee glacé icing. Immediately pipe on a continuous spiral of melted chocolate, keeping the rings evenly spaced. Draw the point of a knife from the edge of the cake to the center, dividing the cake in quarters, then draw the knife from the center to the edge between these lines to create a feathered effect.

For piping chocolate, use a paper pastry bag with the end snipped off, or a pastry bag fitted with a fine writing nozzle. Or, melt the chocolate in a plastic bag and pipe it from the bag. Keep your hand as cool as possible while piping, otherwise the chocolate will become too runny. If the chocolate starts to set in the nozzle, return it to a bowl set over hot water in order to soften it.

Piped decorations. Draw the outline of the required shape on waxed paper as many times as needed. Melt the chocolate and pour into a paper pastry bag. Let stand for a few seconds to cool and thicken slightly, then snip the end of the bag and pipe onto each drawn design. Carefully peel away chocolate from the paper when the chocolate is hard.

Attractive shapes can be made by drawing an outline in dark chocolate, then filling in with milk chocolate when the outline has set. Allow to harden before removing each shape from the paper.

To make trellis cups, turn a muffin pan upside down and cover the pan with plastic wrap, pressing it down between the cups. Pipe a circle around the top and bottom edges of the cups, then pipe a trellis pattern all over each cup, making sure that all the lines connect. When set, carefully lift the trellis cups off the pan and peel away the plastic wrap.

Shapes. Spread a thin layer of melted chocolate onto a sheet of waxed paper. When just set, but not hard, cut out shapes with a cutter or knife.

To cut squares, diamonds, rectangles, and triangles, use a sharp knife dipped into hot water and dried thoroughly. Cut out shapes by pressing straight down without using a sawing motion. For more complex shapes, use a metal cookie cutter dipped into hot water and dried thoroughly. Aspic cutters are ideal for tiny, delicate decorations.

To make chocolate box cakes, cut out squares of thin sponge cake. Spread sides with plain or liqueur-flavored cream and press chocolate squares onto the sides to form a box. The box may be filled with more cream and topped with fruit or nuts.

Very thin chocolate, such as cutout shapes, stales quickly and therefore should not be kept long before

35

using. However, because it is so thin and fragile, it is advisable to keep it in the refrigerator. Providing it is left at room temperature to set and that it is stored in the refrigerator in a covered box and for as short a time as possible, there is little risk of it developing bloom.

Horns. Cream horn pans can be used as molds for chocolate horns. They are attractive as cake decorations, but may also be used as cups for cream, fruit, ice cream, or a truffle mixture. Polish the inside of the cream horn pans with paper towels dusted with cornstarch, then pour in melted chocolate. Tilt the pan until evenly coated and let stand until set, then repeat the process to obtain a thicker layer of chocolate. Let stand until hard, then carefully ease out of the pan.

Cups. Pour cooled melted chocolate into paper cups or petits four cups. Spread chocolate evenly inside the cups with a brush or spoon. Let stand until set, then add another layer of chocolate if desired. Let stand until set hard, then peel away the paper cups. Fill larger ones with fruit and cream or mousse mixtures, smaller ones with nuts or truffle mixtures.

Shells. These make attractive containers for fruit, ice cream, and sorbet. Cover scallop shells with plastic wrap, then brush with an even layer of chocolate. Let stand until hard, then carefully peel away the plastic wrap.

Molding Chocolate

Chocolate molds made of aluminum or plastic are available in a wide variety of shapes and sizes. It is well worth making Easter eggs at home, and it is fun to experiment with different fillings for homemade chocolates.

Before using any chocolate molds, make sure they are absolutely clean, and polish the insides with paper towels dusted with a little cornstarch; make sure all traces of cornstarch are removed before use. This preparation is vital to ensure that the chocolate will remove from the mold easily and that it has a shiny surface.

To make hollow shapes, pour melted chocolate into the mold, then tip the mold from side to side until evenly coated. Pour any excess chocolate back into the bowl. Place the molds hollow-side down on waxed paper and let stand in a cool place (not the refrigerator) until set. Large molds will require two or three coats of chocolate; allow each coat to set before adding the next.

When the chocolate is just beginning to set, gently scrape away any excess from around the rim of the mold. Once the chocolate is completely set, it shrinks away slightly from the mold and is easy to remove. Place the mold hollow-side down, tap gently all over, and the chocolate will drop out easily. Use waxed paper when handling the chocolate, as warm hands will mark the surface.

Easter eggs. To make hollow shapes such as Easter eggs or rabbits, mold two halves and join them together. The easiest way to do this is to heat a baking sheet, then briefly touch the rim of each half against the hot metal. The chocolate will begin to melt and the two halves will seal when touched together. The seam will

39

not be very obvious and can be disguised with piped icing. Decorations, such as eyes on rabbits and names on Easter eggs, can also be piped in icing. Ribbons make an attractive finish.

Homemade chocolates and sweets. Using sheets of chocolate molds, it is possible to produce a selection of impressive homemade chocolates with a variety of fillings. Coat the molds with chocolate as for larger molds. When the chocolate is set, fill the cavity with chopped nuts or a whole nut such as a hazelnut. Dried or glacé fruits that have been soaked in liqueur also make delicious fillings. Fondant centers and marzipan are equally suitable. Once the cavity has been filled, apply a final layer of chocolate to seal in the contents. Let stand until set, then remove from the mold.

Solid shapes are made by simply filling the mold with chocolate and letting it set. Chocolate mice can be given a tail by holding a length of string in place before pouring the chocolate into the mold.

Special effects. A great variety of effects can be achieved by adding colors and flavorings to white chocolate before molding; special oil-

41

based powder colors are available for this purpose. The desired quantity is stirred into the melted chocolate immediately before use.

The quantity of powder required to achieve bold colors, such as red and green, can affect the setting of white chocolate. More successful results can be obtained by using white chocolate-flavored coating and molding buttons; these are available from specialty stores.

Colored animals and fruit shapes, colored appropriately, make attractive cake decorations. Christmas trees are easy to make using green coloring. A striking Santa Claus can be made by using red for his clothes, leaving the fur and beard white, and using semisweet chocolate for his boots. Use the chocolate when it is fairly thick so that it will stay in position. Fill in one color at a time, letting each set before adding the next. This design is ideal as a decoration for a Christmas tree or cake.

Specially formulated powder flavorings are also available. Like the powder colors, they are stirred (sparingly) into the melted chocolate. For example, mint or orange flavors combine well with dark chocolate.

Coating with Chocolate

A wide variety of chocolate-coated sweets and petits fours can be easily produced at home. Chocolate is easier to use for coating and dipping if one tablespoon of vegetable oil is added for every eight ounces of chocolate. The melted chocolate should be at 90°F (32°C) to 95°F (35°C) for coating. Pour the melted chocolate into a narrow container such as a jar or glass to give a good depth of chocolate. Hold whatever is to be coated on a dipping fork or cocktail stick, then dip it into the chocolate. Allow any excess chocolate to run off, then

push the coated candy or fruit off the fork or stick with another fork or cocktail stick onto waxed paper. Let stand in a cool place to set.

Peppermint creams, fudge, toffee, nut brittle, marzipan, fondant, and truffles are delicious half or totally coated in chocolate.

Chocolate-coated fruits are simple but effective. Strawberries and grapes with their stalks intact look particularly attractive half coated, but many other fruits, such as orange sections, kiwi, and pineapple, are suitable. Make sure fruits are clean and completely dry before dipping. Also try glacé, crystallized, and candied fruits such as pineapple, ginger, or strips of orange peel, but wash off the sugary coating and dry them thoroughly first.

Chocolate-coated cherries and marzipan-stuffed dates are delicious served with after-dinner coffee, and nuts such as walnuts and almonds are also enhanced by a chocolate coating.

Selection of chocolate-coated nuts, fresh fruit, candied peel, glacé fruit, truffles, fondants, and stuffed dates

45

Hot Desserts

Chocolate Zabaglione

Makes 4 servings

$^1/_3$ cup sugar
$^1/_4$ cup rum
4 egg yolks
1 oz. semisweet chocolate, finely grated

To Serve:
Ladyfingers (opposite)

◆ Combine sugar, rum, and yolks in a bowl.

♦ Set over a pan of gently simmering water and whisk until thick and mousse-like, 5 to 7 minutes.

♦ Fold in grated semisweet chocolate.

♦ Pour into four glasses and serve immediately with ladyfingers.

Ladyfingers:
♦ Preheat oven to 375°F. Line a baking sheet with baking parchment.

♦ In a large bowl set over a pan of hot water, whisk

49

▼ *Set over a pan of gently simmering water.*

▼ *Whisk until thick and mousse-like.*

3 tablespoons sugar and 1 egg until thick and mousse-like. Carefully fold in $^1/_4$ cup sifted all-purpose flour.

◆ Using a pastry bag fitted with a $^1/_2$-inch plain nozzle, pipe finger lengths of the mixture onto the prepared baking sheet.

◆ Bake in a preheated oven 6 to 8 minutes, until golden.

◆ Cool on a wire rack.

Note: This is a variation of the classic Italian marsala-flavored dessert. It must be served immediately, while still warm.

Italian Baked Peaches
Makes 4 servings

3 oz. amaretti cookies (macaroons), coarsely crushed

1 oz. semisweet chocolate, finely grated

2 tablespoons unsalted butter, softened

4 large peaches

1 tablespoon sugar

♦ Preheat oven to 375°F. Butter a shallow baking dish.

♦ Combine cookie crumbs, grated chocolate, and butter in a medium bowl.

♦ Place peaches in a large bowl and cover with boiling water; let stand 1 minute. Transfer peaches to a large bowl filled with cold water; let stand 1 minute.

♦ Remove, peel carefully, and cut in half. Discard pits.

♦ Using a teaspoon, scoop out a small amount of pulp from each peach half, chop, and add to chocolate mixture.

▼ *Discard pits, scoop out small amount of pulp.*

▼ *Fill each peach half with chocolate filling.*

◆ Fill each peach half with chocolate filling, then sprinkle with sugar.

◆ Bake in preheated oven 30 minutes, until peaches are soft and filling is crisp. Serve hot.

Note: Although the peaches should not be too hard, overripe peaches should be avoided, as they collapse during cooking.

Amaretti cookies are available in Italian delicatessens and some supermarkets. If you cannot find them, use ratafia cookies instead.

Variations: As an alternative to amaretti cookies, ground almonds or hazelnuts may be used.

Either filling may also be used to stuff pears.

Strawberry-Chocolate Crepes
Makes 16 to 18 crepes

Crepes:

1 cup all-purpose flour

1 tablespoon unsweetened cocoa powder

1 tablespoon sugar

2 eggs, beaten

1 3/4 cups milk

2 tablespoons butter, melted

Additional butter, for frying

Crème Pâtissière:

4 egg yolks

1/4 cup sugar

1/4 cup all-purpose flour

1 1/4 cups milk

1 vanilla bean

Filling:

32 to 36 strawberries, hulled and sliced

To Serve:

1 tablespoon Grand Marnier

1 tablespoon confectioners' sugar, sifted

▼ *Cook about 1 minute on each side.*

◆ To prepare crepes, sift flour and cocoa into a large bowl. Stir in sugar, then stir in beaten eggs. Gradually beat in milk and melted butter. Let batter stand at least 2 hours.

◆ Rub bottom of a small skillet with a little butter and heat over medium heat. Pour in 2 tablespoons of batter. Cook about 1 minute on each side. Repeat with remaining batter.

◆ Preheat oven to 350°F.

◆ To prepare crème pâtissière, mix egg yolks, sugar, flour, and a small amount of milk in a medium bowl.

◆ In a small saucepan, heat remaining milk and vanilla bean until almost boiling. Remove vanilla bean; pour milk into egg yolk mixture, stirring constantly.

◆ Return mixture to pan and cook gently, stirring constantly, 2 to 3 minutes.

◆ Place a spoonful of crème pâtissière on a quarter of each crepe. Top with sliced strawberries. Fold crepe in a triangle, enclosing filling.

◆ Arrange crepes in a warmed and buttered ovenproof dish. Cover with foil and heat in oven, 10 to 12 minutes.

◆ Warm Grand Marnier, ignite, and pour over crepes. Dust with confectioners' sugar and serve.

Chocolate Waffles
Makes about 10 waffles

4 tablespoons butter
2 oz. semisweet chocolate
1 1/2 cups all-purpose flour
1 tablespoon baking powder
1 tablespoon plus 2 teaspoons sugar
2 eggs, separated
1 1/4 cups milk
Melted butter

To Serve:
Whipped cream, ground cinnamon, strawberries

◆ Melt butter and chocolate; cool.

◆ Sift flour and baking powder into a large bowl. Stir in sugar. Make a well in center; add egg yolks and mix thoroughly. Gradually add milk, alternating with chocolate and butter mixture. Beat thoroughly.

◆ In a bowl, whisk egg whites until stiff but not dry. Fold egg whites gently into chocolate batter.

◆ Brush a waffle iron with melted butter and set on medium heat. Pour in a small amount of batter and close waffle iron.

◆ Cook about 1 minute on each side or until both sides of the waffle are crisp and golden brown.

◆ Top with whipped cream, sprinkle with cinnamon, and serve hot with strawberries, if desired.

Chocolate Tagliatelle

Makes 4 to 6 servings

Tagliatelle:

2 eggs

About 1 1/2 cups all-purpose flour

2 tablespoons unsweetened cocoa powder

2 tablespoons confectioners' sugar

Sauce:

2 oz. white chocolate

2/3 cup whipping cream

To Decorate:

Semisweet chocolate curls, if desired

◆ To prepare tagliatelle, beat eggs in a large bowl.

◆ Sift the flour, cocoa, and confectioners' sugar over the eggs.

◆ Mix with a fork, then press into a ball with hands. Dough should be firm but pliable and not sticky; add more flour if too moist.

◆ On a lightly floured surface, knead dough

63

mixture firmly for 5 to 10 minutes or until smooth. Wrap in a damp towel and let rest 30 minutes.

◆ Roll out dough on a lightly floured surface. Roll away from you, lifting and stretching dough as you roll, until very thin and smooth.

◆ Spread on a towel and let dry 30 minutes.

◆ Loosely roll up pasta sheet in a cylinder. Using a sharp knife, cut into narrow strips.

◆ Spread over a towel placed over the back of a chair and let rest 20 minutes.

◆ Fill a large saucepan with water; bring to a boil. Cook tagliatelle in boiling water, 3 to 4 minutes or until just tender; drain thoroughly.

A balanced diet consists of items from the five major food groups: dairy, grains, meats, fruits/vegetables, and chocolate.

◆ To prepare sauce, heat white chocolate and whipping cream in a small saucepan over low heat, stirring constantly, until chocolate has melted and sauce is smooth.

◆ Serve tagliatelle with sauce. Garnish with chocolate curls, if desired.

Note: A pasta machine may be used for rolling and cutting tagliatelle, if desired.

Chocolate Fondue
Makes 6 servings

1 pineapple
1 mango
2 kiwifruits
1³/4 cups strawberries
8 oz. seedless green grapes
2 or 3 figs

Fondue:

8 oz. semisweet chocolate, broken in pieces
²/3 cup whipping cream
2 tablespoons brandy

◆ Peel and core pineapple; cut into cubes. Peel mango and slice. Peel kiwifruit and cut into wedges. Cut figs in quarters. Arrange all fruit on six individual plates and chill.

◆ To prepare fondue, place chocolate and whipping cream into a fondue pot.

◆ Heat gently, stirring constantly until chocolate has melted. Stir in brandy; beat until smooth.

67

◆ Place fondue pot over a burner to keep warm. Serve with fruit for dipping.

Variations: For children, substitute orange juice for brandy.

In addition to fruit for dipping, serve small cookies, sponge cakes, or meringues. Almond Fingers (page 336), Ladyfingers (page 49), or meringues from Ginger & Chocolate Meringues (page 295) would be ideal.

Almond Fondue: Use chocolate candy with almonds as an alternative to semisweet chocolate and substitute amaretto for brandy.

Mocha Fondue: Use coffee-flavored chocolate as an alternative to semisweet chocolate and add 3 tablespoons strong coffee. Use Kahlua or Tia Maria in place of brandy.

Orange Fondue: Add juice and the grated peel of half an orange to chocolate and whipping cream before melting chocolate. Use Grand Marnier in place of brandy.

Cranberry & Pecan Cake

Makes 6 to 8 servings

Topping:

4 tablespoons unsalted butter

$^1/_2$ cup sugar

1 (12-oz.) package cranberries

$^1/_2$ cup coarsely chopped pecans

Cake:

3 eggs

$^1/_3$ cup sugar

$^2/_3$ cup self-rising flour

2 tablespoons unsweetened cocoa powder

Pinch of baking powder

$^1/_2$ teaspoon ground cinnamon

3 tablespoons unsalted butter, melted

◆ Preheat oven to 350°F. Place a baking sheet in the preheated oven.

◆ To prepare topping,

71

spread butter over bottom and sides of a 9-inch round cake pan. Coat with sugar.

◆ In a bowl, mix cranberries and pecans; spread evenly over bottom of pan.

◆ To prepare cake, in a bowl set over a pan of hot but not boiling water, whisk eggs and sugar until thick and light and whisk leaves a trail when lifted out of the mixture.

◆ Sift flour, cocoa, baking powder, and cinnamon into a bowl, then sift flour mixture, a small amount at a time, into egg mixture, folding in carefully each time.

◆ Fold in melted butter.

◆ Pour cake mixture over topping. Place pan on heated baking sheet and bake in preheated oven for 40 minutes or until cake is firm and a

I have this theory that chocolate slows down the aging process. It may not be true, but do I dare take the chance?

skewer inserted into center comes out clean.

◆ Let cake cool in pan 10 minutes. Turn out onto a plate and cut in wedges to serve.

Note: This cake may be served hot or cold, but is particularly good served warm with whipped cream. It is best eaten on the day it is made.

Clafoutis aux Cerises et Chocolat

Makes 6 to 8 servings

1 lb. dark sweet cherries, pitted

¼ cup plus 2 tablespoons sugar

3 eggs

½ cup self-rising flour

2 tablespoons unsweetened cocoa powder

⅔ cup whipping cream

1¼ cups milk

2 tablespoons kirsch

Chocolate Cream:

1¼ cups whipping cream

4 oz. semisweet chocolate, broken in pieces

To Decorate:

Confectioners' sugar

◆ Preheat oven to 375°F. Lightly butter a 9-inch flan pan.

◆ Arrange cherries in buttered pan; sprinkle with 2 tablespoons of sugar and set aside.

◆ In a large bowl, whisk eggs and remaining sugar until light and frothy.

◆ Sift flour and cocoa onto a plate; add all at once to egg mixture and beat in thoroughly.

◆ Whisk in whipping cream, then milk and kirsch. Pour batter over cherries.

◆ Bake for 50 to 60 minutes or until slightly risen and set in middle.

◆ Meanwhile, prepare chocolate cream. In a small saucepan, heat whipping cream until almost boiling. Remove from heat and stir in chocolate until completely melted.

◆ Sift confectioners' sugar over clafoutis. Serve warm with chocolate cream.

Variations: Plums, pears, apples, or red or black currants may be used in place of cherries.

There are four basic food groups: milk chocolate, dark chocolate, white chocolate, and chocolate truffles.

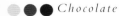

Rum Fudge Pudding
Makes 4 to 6 servings

¹/₂ cup self-rising flour
¹/₄ cup unsweetened cocoa powder
6 tablespoons margarine, softened
¹/₃ cup granulated sugar
1 egg
2 tablespoons dark brown sugar
¹/₂ cup chopped walnuts

Sauce:

1¹/₄ cups hot coffee
2 tablespoons plus 2 teaspoons sugar

3 tablespoons rum

To Serve:
Sifted confectioners' sugar, whipped cream

◆ Preheat oven to 325°F. Grease a 5-cup ovenproof dish.

◆ Sift flour and cocoa into a medium bowl. Add margarine, granulated sugar, and egg and beat thoroughly for about 2 minutes.

◆ Turn into greased dish and sprinkle with brown sugar and chopped walnuts.

◆ To prepare sauce, mix coffee, sugar, and rum in a small bowl. Carefully pour over pudding.

◆ Bake in preheated oven 50 to 60 minutes, until firm to the touch in the center. Sprinkle with confectioners' sugar and serve hot with whipped cream.

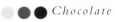

Chocolate Soufflés
Makes 10 soufflés

3 tablespoons unsalted butter
¹/₃ cup all-purpose flour
1 cup milk
4 oz. semisweet chocolate, chopped
1 teaspoon instant coffee granules
¹/₄ cup sugar
3 eggs, separated, plus 1 egg white
2 tablespoons Tia Maria
confectioners' sugar

◆ Preheat oven to 375°F.

◆ Grease ten individual ramekin dishes.

◆ Melt butter in a medium saucepan over low heat. Remove from heat and blend in flour.

◆ Gradually pour in milk, stirring until blended; return to heat. Bring to a boil, stirring constantly, and cook for 3 minutes.

◆ Remove from heat and stir in chocolate, coffee granules, and sugar until melted.

♦ Stir in egg yolks and Tia Maria.

♦ In a large bowl, whisk egg whites until fairly stiff. Using a metal spoon, fold a fourth of the whisked egg whites into the chocolate mixture to lighten; carefully fold in remaining egg whites.

♦ Spoon into greased ramekins.

♦ Bake in preheated oven 20 to 25 minutes, until well risen.

♦ Sprinkle with confectioners' sugar and serve immediately.

▼ *Grease ten individual ramekin dishes.*

▼ *Carefully fold in remaining egg whites.*

Frozen Desserts

Rich Chocolate Ice Cream
Makes 6 to 8 servings

2 eggs plus 2 yolks
^{1}/$_2$ cup sugar
1^1/$_4$ cups half and half
8 oz. semisweet chocolate, chopped
1^1/$_4$ cups whipping cream
^{1}/$_4$ cup dark rum

◆ In a large bowl, combine eggs, yolks, and sugar.

◆ In a large saucepan, heat the half and half and chocolate gently until the chocolate is melted. Stir well to blend, then bring to a boil, stirring constantly.

◆ Pour chocolate mixture into egg mixture, stirring vigorously, then transfer to top of a double boiler or a bowl set over a pan of boiling water.

◆ Cook, stirring constantly, until the custard is thick enough to coat the back of a spoon.

◆ Strain into a bowl and cool.

◆ In a large bowl, whip whipping cream and rum until stiff, then fold into the cooled chocolate mixture.

◆ Pour into a rigid, freezerproof container. Cover, seal, and freeze for about 4 hours, until firm.

◆ Scoop into chilled serving dishes to serve.

Chestnut & Orange Ice Cream
Makes 8 servings

1 can (15^1/$_2$ oz.) unsweetened chestnut puree

2 eggs, separated

Finely grated peel and juice of 1 orange

3 tablespoons Cointreau

2 tablespoons honey

^{1}/$_2$ cup sugar

^{2}/$_3$ cup water

1^1/$_4$ cups whipping cream

Chocolate Sauce:

8 oz. semisweet chocolate, chopped

^{1}/$_4$ cup sugar

^{2}/$_3$ cup water

To Decorate:

Shredded orange peel

◆ In a blender or food processor fitted with a metal blade, process the chestnut puree, egg yolks, orange peel and juice, Cointreau, and honey until smooth.

♦ In a large bowl, whisk egg whites until stiff, then whisk in sugar until glossy and thick.

♦ In a medium bowl, whip cream, then fold into whisked egg whites with chestnut mixture until thoroughly incorporated.

♦ Pour into a rigid, freezerproof container. Cover, seal, and freeze for 4 hours, until solid.

♦ To prepare chocolate sauce, in a small saucepan combine chocolate, sugar, and water and heat gently, stirring frequently until sugar is dissolved.

♦ Bring to a boil and simmer gently for 5 minutes; allow to cool.

♦ Remove ice cream from freezer and let soften slightly, about 15 minutes. Using a melon baller, scoop ice cream in small balls and place on a baking sheet.

◆ Return to freezer for about 30 minutes, until hard.

◆ Pile ice cream balls into chilled serving dishes. Pour chocolate sauce over ice cream balls and decorate with shredded orange peel to serve.

▼ *Avoid the white pith when grating orange peel.*

Malibu Ice Cream
Makes 6 servings

¹/₄ cup cream of coconut

2 eggs, separated

¹/₂ cup sugar

1¹/₄ cups half and half

3 tablespoons Malibu liqueur

²/₃ cup whipping cream

1 recipe Chocolate Sauce, page 89

◆ In a large bowl, blend cream of coconut, egg yolks, and half of the sugar and beat well.

◆ Reserve 2 tablespoons of half and half for decoration. In a small saucepan, bring remaining half and half to a boil, then pour into egg yolk mixture, stirring vigorously.

◆ Return mixture to pan and cook over low heat until slightly thickened; allow to cool. Stir in Malibu.

◆ In a large bowl, whip whipping cream until it holds its shape.

♦ In a small bowl, whisk egg whites until stiff, then whisk in remaining sugar.

♦ Fold whisked egg whites into whipped cream, then fold in coconut custard.

♦ Pour into a rigid, freezerproof container. Cover, seal, and freeze for about 4 hours, until firm.

♦ Using a melon baller, scoop ice cream in small balls and place on a baking sheet.

♦ Return to freezer for 1 hour, until hard. Meanwhile, prepare chocolate sauce.

♦ Pour a pool of chocolate sauce onto each individual serving plate.

◆ Place small dots of the reserved half and half at intervals on surface of chocolate sauce. Using a skewer, swirl in an attractive design.

◆ Arrange ice cream balls in center and serve immediately.

▼ *For variety, experiment with different designs.*

Crème de Menthe Bombes

Makes 6 servings

3 egg yolks
$^1/_2$ cup sugar
1$^1/_4$ cups half and half
2 drops green food coloring
3 tablespoons crème de menthe
1$^1/_4$ cups whipping cream
4 oz. crisp chocolate mints, coarsely chopped

To Serve:
1 recipe Chocolate Sauce, page 89
Frosted mint leaves, page 99

◆ In a medium bowl, beat egg yolks and sugar until creamy.

◆ In a small saucepan, bring half and half to a boil; pour into the egg yolk mixture and mix well.

◆ Transfer to top of a double boiler or a bowl set over a pan of boiling water.

◆ Cook, stirring constantly, until thick enough to coat the back of a spoon.

◆ Strain into a bowl. Stir in food coloring and crème de menthe; allow to cool.

◆ In a large bowl, whip whipping cream until stiff, then whisk in mint custard.

◆ Pour into a rigid, freezerproof container. Cover and freeze for about 3 hours, until half-set.

◆ Stir well and mix in chopped chocolate mints.

◆ Spoon into six ⅔-cup molds. Cover with foil and return to freezer until firm.

◆ Meanwhile, prepare the chocolate sauce.

◆ To serve, dip each mold into warm water to loosen ice cream and place on a chilled plate.

♦ Pour chocolate sauce around each bombe and decorate with frosted mint leaves.

Frosted Mint Leaves: Brush leaves with egg whites, then dip into superfine sugar to coat. Set on waxed paper for 1 to 2 hours to dry.

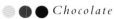

Chocolate-Vanilla Bombes

Makes 8 servings

Chocolate Ice Cream:

1 egg plus 1 yolk

$^1/_4$ cup sugar

$^2/_3$ cup half and half

3 oz. semisweet chocolate, chopped

$^2/_3$ cup whipping cream

2 tablespoons dark rum

Vanilla Ice Cream:

1 egg white

$^1/_4$ cup sugar

$1^1/_4$ cups whipping cream

$^1/_2$ teaspoon vanilla extract

To Serve:

1 recipe Chocolate Sauce, page 89

8 chocolate leaves, page 32

◆ Prepare chocolate ice cream as for Rich Chocolate Ice Cream, page 86.

◆ To prepare vanilla ice cream, in a small

bowl, whisk egg white until stiff, then whisk in sugar.

♦ In a medium bowl, whip whipping cream until thick. Fold in egg white and vanilla.

♦ Divide mixture among eight ¾-cup pudding molds; fill molds about halfway.

♦ Spoon chocolate ice cream mixture over vanilla ice cream.

♦ Place molds on a baking sheet and freeze for about 3 hours, until solid. Cover each mold with foil, seal, and return to freezer until needed.

♦ To serve, dip each mold into warm water and invert bombes onto chilled serving plates. Pour chocolate sauce around each bombe and decorate with a chocolate leaf.

"It's not that chocolates are a substitute for love. Love is a substitute for chocolate. Chocolate is, let's face it, far more reliable than a man."

–Miranda Ingram

 *Chocolate*

Speckled Ice Cream
Makes 8 servings

1 1/2 cups whole-wheat bread crumbs
1/4 cup packed light brown sugar
1 1/4 cups whipping cream
3 egg whites
1/2 cup granulated sugar
2 oz. semisweet chocolate, coarsely grated

To Decorate:
Whipped cream
8 chocolate leaves, page 32

◆ Preheat broiler. Combine bread crumbs and brown sugar on a greased baking sheet.

◆ Broil until golden brown and crisp, stirring frequently; allow to cool. In a medium bowl, lightly whip whipping cream.

◆ In a large bowl, whisk egg whites until stiff; gradually whisk in granulated sugar.

◆ Fold whipped cream into whisked egg

whites with bread crumb mixture and chocolate.

♦ Turn mixture into a 4-cup freezerproof mold or bowl. Cover and freeze for several hours, until firm.

♦ To serve, invert mold or bowl over a plate. Wring out a towel in hot water and place over mold. When towel is cold, wring it out in hot water again and place over mold.

♦ Remove mold. If ice cream has melted on outside, return to freezer for a few minutes.

♦ To decorate, using a pastry bag fitted with a star nozzle, pipe whipped cream on each ice cream serving and top with a chocolate leaf.

Note: This ice cream does not freeze really solid, therefore it is possible to serve it straight from the freezer.

▼ *Combine bread crumbs and brown sugar.*

▼ *Fold other ingredients into whisked egg whites.*

Frozen Praline Ring
Makes 8 servings

Praline:
$^1/_2$ cup sugar
$^1/_2$ cup whole, unblanched almonds

Chocolate Ice Cream:
6 oz. semisweet chocolate, chopped
$^2/_3$ cup half and half
$1^1/_4$ cups whipping cream
2 tablespoons brandy

To Decorate:
Whipped cream

◆ To prepare praline, oil a baking sheet.

◆ In a small, heavy-bottomed saucepan, heat sugar and almonds gently until sugar is melted.

◆ Increase heat and cook until almonds begin to pop and turn brown, shaking pan to ensure

109

almonds are evenly coated with caramel. Pour onto baking sheet and let stand until hard.

♦ To prepare chocolate ice cream, in a small pan, heat chocolate and half and half very gently until chocolate is melted. Stir until smooth; allow to cool.

♦ In a large bowl, whip whipping cream until soft peaks form. Carefully whisk in chocolate mixture and brandy; do not overwhip.

♦ Crush praline with a rolling pin or in a food processor fitted with a metal blade.

♦ Reserve a small amount of praline for decoration. Fold remaining praline into chocolate mixture.

♦ Spoon into a $3^1/3$-cup ring mold. Cover with foil and freeze overnight.

◆ To serve, turn the mold upside down over a chilled plate. Rub mold with a cloth wrung out in very hot water, until the ice cream drops out.

◆ To decorate, using a pastry bag fitted with a star nozzle, pipe whipped cream around top of the ice cream and sprinkle with reserved praline. Cut in slices to serve.

▼ *Crush praline with rolling pin.*

Chocolate & Brandy Bombe
Makes 8 servings

Chocolate Ice Cream:

2 eggs plus 2 yolks

$^1/_2$ cup sugar

1$^1/_4$ cups half and half

8 oz. semisweet chocolate, chopped

1$^1/_4$ cups whipping cream

$^1/_4$ cup brandy

Filling:

$^3/_4$ cup whipping cream

1 tablespoon brandy

1 tablespoon confectioners' sugar

2 oz. meringue cookies, broken into pieces

◆ Prepare chocolate ice cream as for Rich Chocolate Ice Cream, page 86, adding brandy instead of rum.

◆ Freeze for about 4 hours, until firm.

◆ Chill a 6-cup bombe mold or pudding bowl.

▼ *Turn bombe out onto a chilled plate.*

◆ To prepare filling, in a medium bowl, whip whipping cream, brandy, and confectioners' sugar until it stands in stiff peaks. Fold in meringues.

◆ Reserve ¹/₄ cup chocolate ice cream. Line chilled mold or bowl thickly with remaining chocolate ice cream.

◆ Fill center with meringue cream and cover with reserved chocolate ice cream.

The cocoa bean was such a valuable commodity that the Mayans used it as currency.

◆ Cover bombe or bowl with foil and freeze overnight.

◆ To serve, dip mold or bowl in cold water to loosen bombe. Wipe a cloth around the outside, then turn out onto a chilled plate.

◆ Cut in wedges to serve.

Bombe aux Deux Chocolats
Makes 8 servings

Dark Chocolate Ice Cream:

2 eggs plus 2 egg yolks

$1/3$ cup sugar

$1^1/4$ cups half and half

8 oz. semisweet chocolate, chopped

$1^1/4$ cups whipping cream

White Chocolate Ice Cream:

5 oz. white chocolate, chopped

$2/3$ cup milk

$1/4$ cup sugar

$1^1/4$ cups whipping cream

To Decorate:

Chocolate caraque, page 32

◆ Place a 6-cup bombe mold in the freezer.

◆ To prepare dark chocolate ice cream, in a large bowl, beat eggs, egg yolks, and sugar.

◆ In a medium saucepan, heat half and half and chocolate gently until melted.

◆ Bring to a boil, then add to egg mixture. Stir until smooth. Strain into a bowl; cool.

◆ In a medium bowl, whip whipping cream until thick but not too stiff; fold into the chocolate mixture.

◆ Pour into a freezerproof container. Cover and freeze for 1 hour.

◆ Stir well, then refreeze until almost solid.

◆ Line bombe mold with chocolate ice cream. Return to freezer.

◆ In a small saucepan, gently heat white chocolate and half the milk until milk is warm and chocolate is beginning to melt.

◆ Turn off heat. Stir gently until chocolate has melted completely; set aside.

◆ In a large saucepan, heat sugar and remaining milk; allow to cool.

◆ Stir melted chocolate mixture into the sweetened milk.

◆ In a medium bowl, whip whipping cream until thick but not stiff; fold gently into the chocolate mixture.

◆ Fill center of bombe with white chocolate mixture.

◆ Cover and freeze for several hours, until firm.

◆ To serve, dip mold into cold water. Turn out onto a chilled serving dish and decorate with caraque.

Ratafia Tortoni

Makes 8 servings

2 egg whites
$^1/_3$ cup confectioners' sugar
$^2/_3$ cup half and half
$1^3/_4$ cups whipping cream
3 tablespoons medium-dry sherry
4 oz. ratafias or amaretti cookies, crushed
2 oz. semisweet chocolate, grated

To Decorate:
8 ratafias (macaroons)
Whipped cream

◆ In a large bowl, whisk egg whites until stiff, then gradually whisk in confectioners' sugar.

◆ In another large bowl, whisk half and half, whipping cream, and sherry until soft peaks form.

◆ Fold in whisked egg whites.

◆ Reserve $^1/_4$ cup of crushed cookies. Gently fold remaining crushed cookies into cream mixture with grated chocolate. Pour into an 8 x 4-inch loaf pan.

◆ Freeze uncovered until ice cream is frozen around edges; stir with a fork until it reaches a creamy consistency.

◆ Return to freezer and freeze several hours, until firm.

◆ Transfer to refrigerator for 30 minutes before serving to soften slightly.

◆ Turn out of pan. Press reserved crushed cookies over top and sides of tortoni.

◆ Decorate with ratafias, securing them with whipping cream. Cut in slices to serve.

There is nothing better than a good friend—except a good friend with chocolate.

Note: Although traditionally made in a loaf shape, this also may be frozen in a bombe mold or bowl.

Variations: Combine nuts with crushed cookies and substitute brandy or rum for sherry.

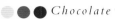

Frozen Vanilla Slice
Makes 8 servings

Chocolate Cake:

2 eggs

$^1/_3$ cup sugar

$^1/_2$ cup all-purpose flour, sifted

3 tablespoons unsweetened cocoa powder, sifted

Vanilla Ice:

1 egg white

$^1/_4$ cup sugar

1 cup whipping cream

$^1/_4$ teaspoon vanilla extract

To Finish:

3 tablespoons crème de cacao

3 tablespoons cold coffee

To Serve:

1 recipe Chocolate Sauce, page 89

◆ Preheat oven to 375°F.

◆ Grease and flour a baking sheet and mark a 13 x 8-inch rectangle.

◆ Prepare cake as for Strawberry Cake, page 229. Spread mixture onto marked rectangle on prepared baking sheet. Bake in preheated oven for 8 minutes.

◆ To prepare vanilla ice, in a medium bowl, whisk egg white until stiff. Whisk in sugar.

◆ In a small bowl, whip whipping cream with vanilla until thick; fold into whisked egg white.

◆ Line an 8 x 4-inch loaf pan with waxed paper.

◆ Cut cake into three equal strips. Lay one piece in the lined loaf pan, trimming to fit.

◆ In a glass measure, combine crème de cacao and coffee and sprinkle a small amount over the cake.

♦ Spread half of the vanilla mixture over top. Place another piece of cake on top, trim to fit, and sprinkle with remaining coffee mixture.

♦ Spread with remaining vanilla ice. Top with remaining piece of cake and trim to fit.

♦ Press down gently, cover with foil, and freeze until solid.

♦ Meanwhile, prepare chocolate sauce.

♦ To serve, dip pan into warm water to loosen the frozen dessert, then turn out onto a flat surface.

♦ Slice with a sharp knife and place slices on chilled individual serving plates.

♦ Spoon chocolate sauce over dessert to serve.

Chocolate-Chestnut Dessert
Makes 10 servings

Cake:
1/3 cup sugar

2 eggs

1/2 cup all-purpose flour, sifted

Chocolate & Chestnut Ice:
8 oz. semisweet chocolate, chopped

1 tablespoon plus 2 teaspoons superfine sugar

2/3 cup half and half

1 can (15 1/2 oz.) unsweetened chestnut puree

1/4 cup brandy

1 1/4 cups whipping cream

To Decorate:
Whipped cream, grated semisweet chocolate

◆ Preheat oven to 375°F. Grease and flour four baking sheets and mark an 8-inch circle on each.

◆ To prepare cake, in a medium bowl, beat sugar and eggs using electric mixer until very thick and mousse-like, and mixture leaves a trail when beaters are lifted.

♦ Carefully fold in flour.

♦ Spread mixture evenly over circles. Bake in preheated oven, two at a time, 6 to 8 minutes, until golden brown.

♦ Using a palette knife, remove from baking sheets and trim each to an 8-inch circle.

♦ To prepare chocolate & chestnut ice, in a small saucepan, gently heat chocolate, sugar, and half and half until chocolate is melted.

♦ In a blender or food processor fitted with a metal blade, process the chocolate mixture, chestnut puree, and brandy until smooth.

♦ Pour into a large bowl and chill.

♦ In a medium bowl, whip whipping cream

until thick, then fold in chestnut mixture.

layering, finishing with chestnut mixture. Cover with foil and freeze until solid.

◆ Lay a cake round in the bottom of a deep, 8-inch, loose-bottom cake pan. Spoon a fourth of the chestnut mixture over the cake round and press down firmly so that the mixture runs down the side of the cake round to form a chocolate edge.

◆ Place a second cake round on top. Repeat

◆ Remove frozen dessert from pan.

◆ Decorate with piped whipped cream and grated chocolate.

◆ Place in refrigerator for 30 minutes before serving to soften. Cut in wedges to serve.

●●● *Chocolate*

Frozen Chocolate-Orange Dessert

Makes 10 servings

Chocolate Cake:

2 eggs

$^1/_3$ cup sugar

$^1/_2$ cup all-purpose flour

1 tablespoon unsweetened cocoa powder

Orange Ice Cream:

Grated peel and juice of 2 oranges

3 eggs, separated

$^2/_3$ cup sugar

1$^1/_4$ cups whipping cream

To Serve:

$^1/_4$ cup Cointreau

1 oz. semisweet chocolate, melted, page 22

◆ Preheat oven to 375°F. Line a deep 8-inch round cake pan with greased waxed paper. Dust with flour.

◆ Prepare cake as for Strawberry Cake, page 229.

◆ Pour into prepared pan and bake in preheated oven for 25 to 30 minutes, until cake springs back when lightly pressed.

◆ Turn out on a wire rack to cool.

◆ To prepare ice cream, in a small bowl, beat orange peel, egg yolks, and half of sugar, using an electric mixer, until smooth.

◆ In another small bowl, whisk egg whites until stiff, then whisk in remaining sugar until thick and glossy.

◆ Whip whipping cream until thick, then whisk in all but $1/4$ cup of orange juice.

◆ Fold in egg yolk mixture, then fold into whisked egg whites.

◆ Mix reserved orange juice with Cointreau.

◆ Split cake in half horizontally; put bottom half in clean cake pan and sprinkle with half of Cointreau mixture.

◆ Spoon half of ice cream mixture over top; cover with remaining cake half.

◆ Press down firmly so mixture runs down side of cake. Sprinkle with remaining Cointreau mixture. Pour remaining ice cream mixture over cake.

◆ Cover with foil and chill overnight.

◆ To serve, dip pan into warm water to loosen frozen dessert and turn out onto a chilled serving plate.

◆ Using a pastry bag fitted with a writing nozzle, drizzle melted chocolate lines over top of dessert.

Frozen Mocha Soufflés

Makes 6 servings

4 eggs, separated
³/4 cup confectioners' sugar, sifted
3 oz. semisweet chocolate, chopped
1 tablespoon instant coffee granules
2 tablespoons water
1¹/4 cups whipping cream
2 tablespoons Kahlua

To Decorate:
Grated semisweet chocolate

♦ Place a double band of foil very tightly around six ramekin dishes to stand 1 inch above the rim of the dishes.

♦ In a large bowl, beat egg yolks and confectioners' sugar until very thick and mousse-like.

♦ In a small saucepan, gently heat chocolate, coffee granules, and water until melted.

◆ Cool slightly, then whisk into egg yolk mixture.

◆ In a medium bowl, whip whipping cream with Kahlua; set aside.

◆ In another medium bowl, whisk the egg whites until stiff, then carefully fold into the chocolate mixture with three fourths of the whipped cream.

◆ Pour into ramekins and freeze overnight.

◆ Remove foil carefully and, using a pastry bag fitted with a star nozzle, pipe remaining whipped cream around the edge of each soufflé.

◆ Decorate with grated chocolate and serve immediately.

▼ *Beat yolks and confectioners' sugar until thick.*

▼ *Whisk in cooled chocolate and coffee mixture.*

Cold Desserts

Chocolate Brandy Creams
Makes 6 servings

3 oz. semisweet chocolate, chopped
²/₃ cup half and half
1¹/₄ cups whipping cream
1 tablespoon confectioners' sugar, sifted
2 tablespoons brandy

To Decorate:
Chocolate curls, page 31

To Serve:
Almond curls, page 144

◆ In a small saucepan, very gently heat chocolate and half and half until chocolate is melted. Stir until smooth; allow to cool.

◆ In a medium bowl, whip whipping cream until thick, then carefully whisk in confectioners' sugar, brandy, and chocolate mixture, taking care not to overwhip.

◆ Spoon into six tall glasses and decorate with chocolate curls.

Chocolate is cheaper than
therapy, and you don't need
an appointment.

◆ Chill until required. Serve with almond curls.

Almond Curls:
◆ Preheat oven to 400°F. Grease and flour two baking sheets.

◆ In a medium bowl, mix ¹/₄ cup sifted all-purpose flour with ¹/₄ cup sugar.

◆ Make a well in center and add an egg white and 2 tablespoons melted butter; mix until smooth.

◆ Drop teaspoonfuls of mixture onto prepared baking sheets. Spread in $2^1/_2$-inch circles and sprinkle with 2 tablespoons sliced almonds.

◆ Bake in preheated oven for 6 to 7 minutes, until pale golden.

◆ Remove with a palette knife and curl around rolling pin. Let stand until firm, then remove.

▼ *Curl circles around rolling pin to shape.*

St. Emilion Dessert

Makes 6 to 8 servings

1 tablespoon brandy
1 tablespoon Amaretto liqueur
6 oz. ratafia cookies (macaroons)
8 tablespoons unsalted butter, softened
¹/2 cup sugar
8 oz. semisweet chocolate, melted, page 22
1¹/4 cups milk
2 eggs, beaten

To Decorate:
Whipped cream
Chocolate leaves, page 32

◆ In a small bowl, mix brandy and Amaretto.

◆ Arrange a layer of cookies in a glass bowl. Sprinkle with half of brandy mixture.

◆ Place remaining cookies on a plate and sprinkle with remaining brandy mixture.

◆ In a medium bowl, cream butter and sugar until light and fluffy. Stir in melted chocolate.

◆ In a medium saucepan, heat milk until almost boiling.

◆ Stir into beaten eggs; return mixture to pan. Stir over gentle heat until mixture thickens and coats back of spoon.

◆ Stir slowly into chocolate mixture. Chill until just beginning to set.

◆ Spoon half of chocolate mixture over cookies in dish. Arrange soaked cookies on top. Cover with remaining chocolate mixture.

◆ Chill several hours or overnight.

◆ Using a pastry bag fitted with a star nozzle, pipe whipped cream on dessert and decorate with chocolate leaves.

Note: This dessert looks attractive when prepared in individual dishes.

Variation: Amaretti cookies may be used in place of ratafias for a more pronounced almond flavor.

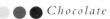 *Chocolate*

Zuccotto

Makes 6 servings

$^3/_4$ cup plus 2 tablespoons self-rising flour

2 tablespoons unsweetened cocoa powder

$^1/_2$ teaspoon baking powder

$^1/_2$ cup sugar

8 tablespoons margarine, softened

2 eggs

3 tablespoons brandy

3 tablespoons cherry brandy

Filling:

$1^1/_4$ cups whipping cream

2 tablespoons confectioners' sugar, sifted

$^1/_2$ cup chopped hazelnuts, toasted

8 oz. dark sweet cherries, pitted

2 oz. semisweet chocolate, grated or finely chopped

To Decorate:

1 tablespoon unsweetened cocoa powder

1 tablespoon confectioners' sugar

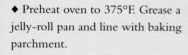

♦ Preheat oven to 375°F. Grease a jelly-roll pan and line with baking parchment.

♦ Sift flour, cocoa, and baking powder into a large bowl. Add sugar, margarine, and eggs.

♦ Beat thoroughly until well mixed; pour into prepared pan.

♦ Bake in preheated oven, 15 to 20 minutes or until well risen and firm to the touch.

♦ Turn out onto a wire rack to cool.

♦ Using the rim of a 5-cup pudding bowl as a guide, cut a circle from the cake.

♦ Line bowl with plastic wrap, then with remaining cake, cutting as needed to fit.

◆ In a small bowl, mix brandy and cherry brandy. Sprinkle over the cake in the bowl and the cake round.

◆ To prepare filling, in a medium bowl, whip the whipping cream and confectioners' sugar until stiff.

◆ Fold in hazelnuts, cherries, and chocolate.

◆ Fill cake-lined bowl with cream mixture.

◆ Press cake round on top. Cover with a plate and a weight. Chill several hours or overnight.

◆ Turn out onto a serving plate.

◆ Decorate with cocoa and confectioners' sugar, sifted over the top.

Chocolate Christmas Pudding

Makes 10 to 12 servings

$^1/_3$ cup glacé pineapple, coarsely chopped

$^1/_3$ cup chopped glacé cherries

$^1/_3$ cup raisins

Peel of $^1/_2$ orange, if desired

3 tablespoons brandy

3 tablespoons half and half

12 oz. semisweet chocolate, chopped

$^1/_2$ cup cream cheese, softened

4 oz. ratafia cookies (macaroons), broken into pieces

To Serve:

Whipped cream

Grated semisweet chocolate

♦ Grease a 4-cup pudding bowl.

♦ In a small bowl, combine pineapple, cherries, raisins, and orange peel, if desired. Pour brandy over fruit.

♦ In a medium saucepan, very gently heat the half and half and chocolate until melted. Stir until smooth.

♦ Add fruit with brandy; cool.

♦ In a large bowl, beat cream cheese with a small amount of chocolate mixture until smooth, then beat in the remaining chocolate mixture.

♦ Mix in cookies and pour into the greased pudding bowl. Chill overnight.

♦ To serve, turn out onto a chilled plate.

◆ Spoon some of whipped cream over the pudding and let it trickle down the sides; serve remaining whipped cream separately.

◆ Sprinkle pudding with grated chocolate.

Note: This pudding is extremely rich. Serve it cut in thin slices.

 *Chocolate*

Steamed Chocolate Pudding

Makes 4 to 6 servings

8 tablespoons unsalted butter, softened
¹/₂ cup sugar
¹/₂ teaspoon ground cinnamon
4 eggs, separated
4 oz. semisweet chocolate, melted, then cooled
1 tablespoon brandy
²/₃ cup whipping cream
¹/₄ cup crème fraîche

◆ Lightly oil a 4-cup pudding bowl.

◆ Pour enough water into a large, deep saucepan to come a third of the way up the side of the bowl; bring to a boil.

◆ In a large bowl, cream butter, sugar, and cinnamon until pale and thick. Beat in egg yolks, one at a time.

◆ Carefully stir in cooled melted chocolate and brandy.

◆ In another large bowl, whisk egg whites until stiff.

◆ Stir a small amount of egg whites into the chocolate mixture; carefully fold in remaining egg whites.

◆ Spoon the chocolate mixture into the oiled pudding bowl. Cover with oiled foil or a double layer of greased waxed paper and tie securely with string.

◆ Place bowl in pan of boiling water. Cover pan and simmer gently for 45 minutes.

◆ Let pudding stand in bowl until completely cool; turn out onto serving dish.

◆ In a small bowl, whisk whipping cream and crème fraîche.

◆ Decorate pudding with whipped cream mixture or serve separately, if desired.

▼ *Simmer pudding gently for 45 minutes.*

Note: The pudding will sink slightly when removed from the heat. This is normal and contributes to the rather dense, rich texture.

Variation: Cook in individual pudding molds for 25 to 30 minutes. Remove and decorate with piped whipped cream mixture and chocolate hearts.

Raspberry-Chocolate Brûlées
Makes 6 to 8 servings

8 oz. fresh raspberries or strawberries
2 tablespoons framboise or strawberry liqueur
2 cups whipping cream
4 oz. semisweet chocolate, melted, then cooled
1/2 cup packed light brown sugar

To Decorate:
Mint leaves
12 to 16 fresh raspberries or strawberries

◆ Spread raspberries or strawberries over bottom of six to eight 2/3-cup freezerproof ramekin dishes. Sprinkle with framboise.

◆ In a large bowl, whip whipping cream until it begins to hold its shape.

◆ Add cooled chocolate and continue whipping until cream is stiff.

◆ Spread over raspberries. Place in freezer until cream is frozen.

◆ Preheat broiler.

◆ Sprinkle brown sugar thickly over cream.

◆ Broil until sugar is melted and caramelized.

◆ Refrigerate brûlées until fruit and cream have thawed.

◆ Serve the same day, decorated with mint leaves and fresh raspberries or strawberries.

Note: If you are short of time, it is not necessary to freeze the brûlées before broiling, but it does prevent the cream from bubbling up through the sugar during broiling.

Always ensure broiler is preheated before broiling brûlées to caramelize brown sugar.

Variation: Use red currants or sliced peaches instead of raspberries or strawberries. Fresh fruit gives a better result than frozen fruit.

Chocolate Terrine

Makes 6 to 8 servings

White Chocolate Mousse:

2/3 cup whipping cream

2 eggs, separated

2 tablespoons sugar

4 oz. white chocolate, melted, then cooled

*1/4-oz. envelope unflavored gelatin (about
    1 tablespoon) dissolved in 3 tablespoons water*

Dark Chocolate Mousse:

2/3 cup whipping cream

2 eggs, separated

1 tablespoon plus 2 teaspoons sugar

4 oz. semisweet chocolate, melted, then cooled

*1/4-oz. envelope unflavored gelatin, (about
    1 tablespoon) dissolved in 3 tablespoons water*

Orange Cream:

2 tablespoons sugar

1 tablespoon cornstarch

2/3 cup milk

2 egg yolks, lightly beaten

1 tablespoon Cointreau

*¹/₄ cup frozen thawed orange juice
    concentrate*
²/₃ cup whipping cream

To Decorate:
Chocolate-dipped orange sections, page 43

◆ To prepare white chocolate mousse, whip whipping cream in a small bowl.

◆ In another small bowl, whisk egg whites until fairly stiff.

◆ In a third bowl, whisk egg yolks with sugar until thick and pale.

◆ Stir in cooled chocolate, then gelatin and then whipped cream.

◆ Gently fold in whisked egg whites. Pour mixture into an oiled 8 x 4-inch loaf pan.

◆ Freeze until firm.

◆ Prepare dark chocolate mousse in same way.

◆ Pour over white chocolate mousse. Chill for 2 hours or until set.

◆ To prepare orange cream, in a saucepan, combine sugar, cornstarch, and 2 tablespoons of milk; stir in remaining milk.

◆ Cook over low heat until thickened, stirring. Whisk yolks into mixture; cool.

◆ Stir in Cointreau, orange juice, and cream.

◆ Turn out terrine. Serve in slices, surrounded by orange cream.

◆ Decorate with chocolate orange sections.

 *Chocolate*

Coeurs à la Crème au Chocolat
Makes 8 servings

1 cup cottage cheese or ricotta cheese
¹/₃ cup confectioners' sugar, sifted
1¹/₄ cups whipping cream
2 oz. semisweet chocolate, grated
2 egg whites

Chocolate Cream Sauce:
²/₃ cup half and half
2 oz. semisweet chocolate, melted

◆ Line eight individual coeurs à la crème molds with cheesecloth, or line a sieve with cheesecloth.

◆ Press cheese through a sieve into a large bowl.

◆ Add confectioners' sugar and whipping cream and beat thoroughly.

◆ Stir in grated chocolate.

◆ In a small bowl, whisk egg whites until stiff but not dry. Lightly fold into cheese mixture.

◆ Spoon mixture into molds or prepared sieve. Refrigerate overnight to drain.

◆ To prepare chocolate cream sauce, pour a fourth of the half and half in a small bowl. Stir in the melted chocolate.

◆ Reserve 1 tablespoon of remaining half and half. Gradually stir remaining half and half into chocolate mixture; stir until smooth.

◆ Turn out each coeur à la crème onto a plate and pour chocolate cream around it.

◆ To decorate, drop dots of reserved half and half onto sauce and, using a skewer, feather in a design. If crème has been made in sieve, turn onto a serving dish and serve chocolate cream separately.

Variation: Coeurs à la crème may be served with fruit, such as raspberries or strawberries, or with fruit puree as a sauce instead of chocolate cream.

▼ *Line the molds with cheesecloth.*

Chocolate-Orange Cups
Makes 4 to 6 servings

8 oz. semisweet chocolate, chopped
1 1/4 cups half and half
Grated peel of 1 orange
2 tablespoons brandy
2 tablespoons whipping cream

◆ In a medium saucepan, very gently heat chocolate, half the half and half, and grated orange peel, stirring constantly until melted.

◆ Stir in remaining half and half and brandy and pour into six cups or small ramekins.

◆ Pipe a continuous whirl of whipping cream from center to edge of chocolate cups. Using a skewer, make a feathered design.

◆ Chill 2 to 3 hours, until set.

Note: Do not allow chocolate mixture to set before piping whipping cream or you will not be able to create a feathered effect.

White Chocolate Mousse
Makes 6 servings

²/₃ cup whipping cream

2 egg whites

3 tablespoons unsalted butter, softened

6 oz. white chocolate, melted, page 22

1 teaspoon triple-strength rose water

4 oz. semisweet chocolate, melted, then cooled

To Decorate:

Crystallized rose petals, page 178

♦ In a small bowl, whip whipping cream until thick but not stiff.

♦ In another small bowl, whisk egg whites until stiff but not dry. Set both aside.

♦ In a large bowl, beat butter into melted white chocolate until smooth and creamy.

♦ Cool, but do not allow to set. Gently fold in whipped cream.

♦ Stir in rose water, then fold in whisked egg whites.

♦ Spoon mixture into six ²/₃-cup ramekins or cups. Cover and chill until set.

♦ Spread cooled melted semisweet chocolate evenly over mousses.

♦ Decorate with crystallized rose petals.

♦ Refrigerate until chocolate has hardened before serving.

Crystallized Rose Petals: Brush dry rose petals with egg white, dip into superfine sugar, and set on waxed paper to dry. Store in an airtight container up to three days, until needed.

If desired, use other flower petals. Crystallized violets and primroses are particularly attractive.

"Nine out of ten people
like chocolate.
The tenth person always lies."
–John Q. Tullius

Variation: Mousses can be made with semisweet chocolate, flavored with rum or brandy instead of rose water, and topped with a layer of white chocolate.

Chocolate-Strawberry Cones

Makes 12 cones

3 tablespoons all-purpose flour

1 tablespoon unsweetened cocoa powder

¹/4 cup sugar

1 egg white

2 tablespoons unsalted butter, melted

2 tablespoons chopped pistachios

Filling:

1 cup whipping cream

2 tablespoons framboise

4 oz. strawberries, hulled

◆ Preheat oven to 400°F. Grease and flour three baking sheets.

◆ Sift flour and cocoa into a medium bowl; stir in sugar.

◆ Make a well in center. Add egg white and butter and beat until smooth.

◆ Place spoonfuls of mixture onto prepared baking sheets, spacing well apart, and spread

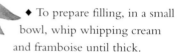

out thinly to 4-inch circles.

♦ Sprinkle with nuts.

♦ Bake in preheated oven for 4 to 6 minutes.

♦ Remove with a palette knife and curl each around a cornet mold, holding in position until set. Remove from molds.

♦ To prepare filling, in a small bowl, whip whipping cream and framboise until thick.

♦ Spoon a fourth of the whipped cream into a pastry bag fitted with a large, fluted nozzle.

♦ Slice strawberries and reserve twelve slices. Fold remaining strawberry slices into remaining whipped cream and spoon into chocolate cones.

◆ Pipe a rosette of whipped cream on each and decorate with a strawberry slice.

Note: This mixture makes fifteen cones, which allows for three breakages. Only bake three circles at a time or they will begin to set before you have time to roll them up.

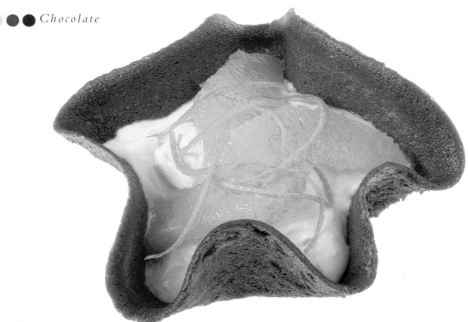

Cointreau Cream in Tulips
Makes 6 servings

3 tablespoons all-purpose flour

1 tablespoon unsweetened cocoa powder

1/4 cup sugar

1 egg white

2 tablespoons unsalted butter, melted

Filling:

2 oranges

1 cup cottage cheese

2 tablespoons honey

2 tablespoons Cointreau

2/3 cup whipping cream

◆ Preheat oven to 400°F. Grease and flour three baking sheets.

◆ Sift flour and cocoa into a medium bowl; stir in sugar. Make a well in center. Add egg white and butter and beat until smooth.

◆ Drop spoonfuls of mixture onto prepared baking sheets and spread out thinly in 4-inch circles. Bake in preheated oven for 4 to 6 minutes.

◆ Remove from baking sheets and place each cookie, top-side down, over bottom of an inverted glass.

◆ Mold cookie to give wavy edges. Let stand until hard, then carefully remove cookie.

◆ To prepare filling, pare two strips of peel

from an orange. Cut in fine shreds and blanch in boiling water for 1 minute. Drain on paper towels and set aside.

◆ Finely grate peel from the other orange. Peel and section both oranges, discarding all pith and seeds.

◆ In a medium bowl, combine cottage cheese, honey, grated orange peel, and Cointreau.

◆ In another bowl, whip cream until soft peaks form, then fold into cheese mixture.

◆ Spoon filling into six tulip cups and decorate with orange sections and orange shreds.

Note: The cookie mixture will make nine tulips, which allows for three breakages.

▼ *Mold cookie to give wavy edges.*

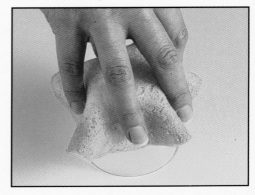

Chocolate Meringue Nests
Makes 8 nests

1 tablespoon unsweetened cocoa powder
¹/₂ cup sugar
2 egg whites

Filling:
¹/₂ cup whipping cream
2 tablespoons crème de cacao
6 chocolate hearts, page 34

◆ Preheat oven to 275°F. Line a baking sheet with baking parchment and mark eight 3-inch

circles on it. Sift cocoa and 1 tablespoon of sugar together; set aside.

◆ In a small bowl, whisk egg whites until stiff and dry-looking. Gradually whisk in remaining sugar until thick and glossy, then carefully fold in cocoa mixture.

◆ Using a pastry bag fitted with a ¹/₄-inch fluted nozzle, pipe over each circle, starting from the center and working to the edge, forming a bottom. Pipe on top of outside edge, forming a nest.

◆ Bake in preheated oven for $1^1/_2$ hours, until dry; cool.

◆ In a small bowl, whip whipping cream and crème de cacao until thick. Spoon flavored cream into each meringue nest and decorate with chocolate hearts.

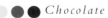 *Chocolate*

Hazelnut Galette with Kumquats

Makes 8 servings

1 lb. kumquats, halved lengthwise

$^3/_4$ cup sugar

$1^1/_4$ cups water

$^2/_3$ cup whipping cream

Pastry:

6 tablespoons butter, softened

$^1/_4$ cup sugar

$^3/_4$ cup all-purpose flour

$^1/_4$ cup unsweetened cocoa powder

$^3/_4$ cup ground hazelnuts

To Decorate:

Confectioners' sugar

◆ Preheat oven to 375°F.

◆ Place kumquats in a large saucepan with sugar and water. Bring to a boil, then simmer gently for 30 minutes. Drain and cool.

◆ Meanwhile, prepare pastry in a large bowl. Cream butter and sugar until light and fluffy.

◆ Sift in flour and cocoa. Add ground hazelnuts and mix thoroughly to make a firm dough.

◆ Knead lightly on a floured surface until smooth. Divide dough in half and roll each piece into an 8-inch round on a baking sheet.

◆ Bake in preheated oven, 15 to 20 minutes or until firm.

◆ Cut a round into eight wedges while still warm. Transfer remaining round and wedges to wire racks to cool.

◆ In a small bowl, whip whipping cream. Spread three fourths of the whipped cream over the hazelnut round.

◆ Reserve three kumquats; arrange remainder on whipped cream.

◆ Place hazelnut wedges on top and sift confectioners' sugar over wedges.

◆ Using a pastry bag fitted with a star nozzle, pipe a rosette of remaining whipped cream on each wedge.

◆ Cut reserved kumquats in pieces and place a piece on each rosette. Serve immediately.

Variation: To prepare individual galettes, cut rolled-out pastry into eight 3-inch rounds for bottoms and eight 2-inch rounds for tops. Bake 12 to 15 minutes. Assemble as above.

Profiteroles with Liqueur Cream

Makes 6 servings

Choux Pastry:

4 tablespoons unsalted butter or margarine

²/₃ cup water

¹/₃ cup all-purpose flour, sifted

2 eggs

Filling:

³/₄ cup whipping cream

2 tablespoons crème de cacao

To Serve:

1 recipe Chocolate Sauce, page 89

◆ Preheat oven to 425°F. In a large pan, melt butter or margarine. Add water and bring to a boil. Add flour all at once and beat thoroughly until mixture leaves sides of pan.

◆ Cool slightly, then vigorously beat in eggs, one at a time.

♦ In a pastry bag fitted with a plain $^1/_2$-inch nozzle, pipe small mounds of pastry onto a dampened baking sheet.

♦ Bake in preheated oven 10 minutes. Reduce temperature to 375°F and bake 20 to 25 minutes more, until golden.

♦ Make a slit in side of each profiterole and cool on a wire rack.

♦ To prepare filling, in a small bowl, whip whipping cream and crème de cacao until thick.

♦ In a pastry bag fitted with a plain $^1/_8$-inch nozzle, pipe filling into each profiterole.

♦ Pile profiteroles in pyramids on individual serving dishes. Pour chocolate sauce over profiteroles just before serving.

▼ *Beat until pastry mixture leaves sides of pan.*

▼ *Pipe small mounds onto prepared baking sheet.*

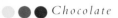

Chocolate-Chestnut Tart
Makes 6 to 8 servings

8 oz. gingersnap cookies, crushed
6 tablespoons butter, melted

Filling:
³/4 cup unsweetened chestnut puree, page 201
¹/4 cup sugar
Few drops vanilla extract
³/4 cup ricotta cheese
2 eggs
3¹/2 oz. semisweet chocolate, melted, page 22
¹/4 cup ground almonds

To Decorate:
²/3 cup whipping cream, whipped
Chocolate shapes, page 34

◆ Preheat oven to 350°F.

◆ In a small bowl, combine cookie crumbs and melted butter. Press onto bottom and up sides of a 9-inch, loose-bottomed flan pan.

◆ Bake in preheated oven 10 minutes; cool.

◆ To prepare filling, in a small bowl, beat chestnut puree, sugar, and vanilla until smooth.

◆ In a medium bowl, beat ricotta cheese and eggs until smooth.

◆ Stir melted chocolate into cheese mixture. Add chestnut puree mixture and mix thoroughly. Stir in ground almonds.

◆ Pour filling into prepared crust and bake in preheated oven for 35 minutes or until lightly set. Cool, then chill thoroughly.

◆ To decorate, spread a thin layer of whipped cream over top and sprinkle with grated chocolate.

◆ Using a pastry bag fitted with a star nozzle, pipe remaining whipped cream around edge and decorate with chocolate diamonds. Serve immediately.

Note: If unsweetened chestnut puree is unavailable, the sweetened version may be used. Omit sugar and vanilla from recipe, as sweetened chestnut puree usually tastes quite strongly of vanilla, and expect a sweeter result.

To make chestnut puree:

◆ Remove both the outer and inner skins; make a slit near the pointed end, put in a saucepan of boiling water, and leave for 2 to 3 minutes before peeling.

◆ Put chestnuts in a clean saucepan and cover with a mixture of half milk and half water. Cover and simmer for 20 to 30 minutes or until soft.

◆ Drain and sieve. Blend in a food processor to a smooth puree.

Rum & Raisin Cheesecake

Makes 8 servings

¹/₃ cup raisins

¹/₄ cup dark rum

4 tablespoons unsalted butter or margarine

8 graham crackers, crushed

3 oz. semisweet chocolate, chopped

2 tablespoons milk

1 cup cottage cheese

2 eggs, separated

*1²/₃ (¹/₄-oz.) envelopes unflavored gelatin
(5 teaspoons) soaked in 3 tablespoons water*

²/₃ cup whipping cream

¹/₄ cup sugar

To Finish:

Chocolate caraque, page 32

◆ In a small bowl, soak raisins in rum for 2 to 3 hours.

◆ Grease an 8-inch springform cake pan.

◆ Melt butter or margarine in a small

saucepan, then stir in graham cracker crumbs until well mixed.

♦ Press mixture over bottom of greased pan. Let stand until hard.

♦ In a small saucepan, gently heat chocolate and milk until chocolate is melted.

♦ In a large bowl, mix cottage cheese and egg yolks until smooth.

♦ Gradually beat in chocolate mixture and rum and raisins.

♦ In a small saucepan, gently heat gelatin until dissolved.

♦ In a small bowl, whip whipping cream until thick.

♦ Fold gelatin and whipped cream into chocolate mixture.

Coffee . . . chocolate . . . men . . . some things are just better when they're rich!

- ◆ In a small bowl, whisk egg whites until stiff.

- ◆ Whisk in sugar; fold into chocolate mixture.

- ◆ Spoon over crust and chill until set.

- ◆ Remove cheesecake from pan and transfer to a serving plate.

- ◆ Decorate with chocolate caraque.

Chocolate-Orange Cheesecake

Makes 8 servings

4 tablespoons unsalted butter
8 graham crackers
2 tablespoons light brown sugar
1 cup cottage cheese
2 eggs, separated
Grated peel of 1 orange
8 oz. semisweet chocolate, melted, page 22
2 tablespoons Cointreau
$^2/_3$ cup whipping cream
1 tablespoon plus 2 teaspoons granulated sugar

♦ Grease an 8-inch springform cake pan.

♦ In a small saucepan, melt butter, then stir in graham cracker crumbs and brown sugar.

♦ Press over bottom of pan; chill until firm.

♦ In a medium bowl, mix cottage cheese, egg yolks, and orange peel until smooth. Add melted chocolate and Cointreau and mix until evenly blended.

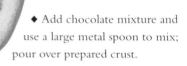

♦ In a small bowl, whip whipping cream until thick.

♦ Reserve 2 tablespoons for decoration; fold remaining cream into cheese mixture.

♦ In a large bowl, whisk egg whites until stiff.

♦ Whisk in granulated sugar until thick.

♦ Add chocolate mixture and use a large metal spoon to mix; pour over prepared crust.

♦ Spoon dots of reserved whipped cream all over cheesecake.

♦ Run a skewer through dots to create a feathered design.

♦ Chill 2 to 3 hours, until set.

▼ *Stir cracker crumbs and sugar into melted butter.*

▼ *Press mixture over bottom of greased pan.*

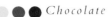

Chocolate & Pistachio Marquise
Makes 8 servings

$^1/_3$ cup strong coffee

2 tablespoons brandy

32 ladyfingers

6 tablespoons unsalted butter, softened

$^1/_3$ cup sugar

2 egg yolks

1 cup whipping cream

6 oz. semisweet chocolate, melted, page 22

$^1/_4$ cup pistachios, coarsely chopped

Raspberry Sauce:

8 oz. raspberries

$^1/_3$ cup confectioners' sugar

1 tablespoon water

1 teaspoon lemon juice

To Decorate:

Mint leaves

◆ Line a 9 x 5-inch loaf pan with plastic wrap.

◆ In a shallow dish, combine coffee and brandy. Dip ladyfingers in briefly and line prepared pan, cutting to fit if necessary.

◆ In a large bowl, beat butter and half of the sugar until thick and pale.

◆ In a small bowl, whisk egg yolks with remaining sugar until thick and pale.

◆ In a third bowl, lightly whip the whipping cream.

◆ Stir cooled melted chocolate into butter mixture.

◆ Stir in egg mixture and fold in whipped cream. Carefully fold in pistachios.

◆ Pour into prepared pan and smooth top.

◆ Chill several hours or overnight.

◆ To prepare raspberry sauce, in a blender or food processor fitted with a metal blade, process raspberries, confectioners' sugar, and water to a puree.

◆ Press through a sieve into a bowl. Stir in lemon juice.

◆ Turn out marquise onto a flat plate. Cut in slices and serve with raspberry sauce.

◆ Decorate with mint leaves.

Marbled Chiffon Pie
Makes 8 servings

Almond Pastry:

1$^1/_2$ cups all-purpose flour

2 teaspoons sugar

$^1/_2$ cup ground almonds

8 tablespoons butter, chilled

1 egg yolk

Few drops almond extract

2 teaspoons water

Chocolate Filling:

1$^1/_4$ cups milk

3 eggs, separated

$^1/_2$ cup sugar

1$^2/_3$ ($^1/_4$-oz.) envelopes unflavored gelatin
  (5 teaspoons) soaked in 2 tablespoons water

2 oz. semisweet chocolate, chopped

2 oz. white chocolate, chopped

◆ To prepare almond pastry, sift flour into a bowl. Stir in sugar and almonds.

◆ Cut in butter until mixture resembles bread crumbs. Stir in egg yolk, almond extract, and water.

◆ Knead lightly, then chill for 30 minutes.

◆ Preheat oven to 400°F.

◆ On a lightly floured surface, roll out pastry and line a 9-inch loose-bottomed flan pan.

◆ Bake blind 20 to 25 minutes, until crisp and golden; allow to cool.

◆ To prepare chocolate filling, in a small saucepan, heat milk until almost boiling.

◆ In a medium bowl, mix yolks and sugar.

◆ Gradually pour in hot milk, stirring constantly. Return to pan; stir over low heat until custard begins to thicken.

◆ Remove from heat and add gelatin; stir until dissolved.

◆ Divide custard in half. Add semisweet chocolate to one half and white chocolate to other half; stir until smooth; cool.

◆ In a small bowl, whisk egg whites until soft peaks form.

◆ Fold half of whisked egg whites into cooled semisweet chocolate mixture and remaining half into white chocolate mixture.

◆ When chocolate mixtures are beginning to set, pour into pastry in strips.

◆ Using a fork, swirl two chocolate mixtures together to give a marbled effect.

◆ Chill until completely set.

Cakes

Chocolate

Chocolate Praline Cake
Makes 10 to 12 servings

Praline:
$1/2$ cup sugar
$1/2$ cup whole, unblanched almonds

Meringue Rounds:
5 egg whites
$1^1/4$ cups sugar
$1^1/3$ cups ground almonds

Chocolate Butter Cream:
8 tablespoons unsalted butter, softened

$1^1/4$ cups confectioners' sugar, sifted
1 tablespoon water
3 oz. semisweet chocolate, melted, page 22

To Finish:
2 oz. semisweet chocolate, melted

♦ Prepare praline as for Frozen Praline Ring, page 109. Grind finely in a food processor.

♦ Preheat oven to 350°F. Line five baking

sheets with baking parchment
and mark with
an 8-inch circle.

◆ Using sharp knife, trim each
circle while still warm, then
transfer to a wire rack to cool.

◆ To prepare meringue rounds, whisk egg
whites until stiff, then fold in sugar and
ground almonds.

◆ To prepare butter cream, in a medium
bowl, beat butter and half of the confectioners'
sugar until creamy.

◆ Spread mixture onto baking sheets and bake
in preheated oven for 15 to 20 minutes.

◆ Add remaining confectioners' sugar and
water; beat until smooth. Stir in melted
chocolate.

Life is like a box of chocolates . . . full of nuts!

◆ Mix half of praline with butter cream and sandwich meringues together.

◆ Spread side of cake with butter cream and cover with remaining praline. Spread remaining butter cream over top of cake.

◆ In a pastry bag fitted with a writing nozzle, drizzle melted chocolate over top of cake.

Note: If you don't have enough baking sheets, use those you have in rotation. Cool meringue rounds slightly, invert onto a flat surface, and peel off lining paper.

Chocolate Caramel Cake
Makes 10 to 12 servings

4 eggs
³/₄ cup sugar
1¹/₄ cups all-purpose flour, sifted
1¹/₂ recipes Chocolate Butter Cream, page 221
2 oz. semisweet chocolate, grated

Caramel:
²/₃ cup water
²/₃ cup sugar

◆ Preheat oven to 375°F. Grease and flour

six baking sheets and mark an 8-inch circle
on each.

◆ In a medium bowl, beat egg and sugar, using
an electric mixer, until very thick and mousse-
like and a trail is left when beaters
are lifted, about 7 minutes.

◆ Using a metal spoon, carefully fold in flour.

◆ Spread mixture onto prepared baking sheets

and bake in preheated oven 6 to 8 minutes, until golden brown.

♦ Using a sharp knife, trim each round while still warm, then transfer to a wire rack to cool.

♦ Place one round on an oiled baking sheet.

♦ To prepare caramel, in a small saucepan, combine water and sugar and heat very gently until sugar is dissolved.

♦ Bring to a boil and cook rapidly until dark brown.

♦ Pour immediately over the round on the baking sheet. Let stand until just about set.

♦ Using an oiled knife, cut ten to twelve sections and trim around edges.

♦ Reserve a small amount of butter cream. Sandwich remaining rounds together with butter cream, placing the caramel-covered round on top.

◆ Spread side with butter cream and coat with grated chocolate.

◆ Using a pastry bag fitted with a large, fluted nozzle, pipe a rosette of reserved butter cream on each section.

Note: If you don't have six baking sheets, use those you have in rotation, greasing and flouring each time.

Strawberry Cake
Makes 8 servings

Chocolate Cake:

3 eggs

$^1/_2$ cup sugar

$^3/_4$ cup all-purpose flour, sifted

2 tablespoons unsweetened cocoa powder, sifted

To Finish:

8 oz. strawberries

1$^1/_4$ cups whipping cream

1 tablespoon confectioners' sugar

2 tablespoons kirsch

Chocolate curls, page 31

◆ Preheat oven to 275°F. Grease and line a deep, 9-inch round cake pan.

◆ To prepare cake, beat eggs and sugar in a medium bowl, using an electric mixer, until thick and mousse-like and a trail is left when beaters are lifted.

◆ Sift flour and cocoa powder together.

♦ Using a metal spoon, carefully fold into beaten egg mixture.

♦ Spoon into prepared pan and bake for 25 to 30 minutes, until cake springs back when lightly pressed in center.

♦ Turn out onto a wire rack to cool.

♦ To finish, reserve four strawberries. Hull and slice the remaining strawberries.

♦ In a medium bowl, whip whipping cream with confectioners' sugar until thick; reserve two thirds of the whipped cream.

♦ Fold sliced strawberries into remaining whipped cream.

♦ Cut cake in layers and sprinkle each layer with 1 tablespoon of kirsch.

♦ Place one layer on a serving plate and cover

with strawberry cream mixture. Place other layer on top.

♦ Cover top and sides of cake with strawberry cream; swirl top in a decorative pattern and coat sides with chocolate curls.

♦ Using a pastry bag fitted with a fluted nozzle, pipe a decorative border of reserved whipped cream around the top of the cake.

♦ Arrange reserved strawberries to finish.

231

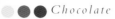

Sacher Torte
Makes 8 to 10 servings

3 tablespoons coffee

6 oz. semisweet chocolate, chopped

2 tablespoons unsalted butter or margarine, softened

²/₃ cup sugar

5 eggs, separated

1¹/₄ cups all-purpose flour, sifted

Filling:

¹/₄ cup apricot jam

1 tablespoon water

Icing:

6 oz. semisweet chocolate, chopped

2 tablespoons half and half

◆ Preheat oven to 325°F. Grease a deep, 9-inch round cake pan and line with baking parchment.

◆ In a small saucepan, gently heat coffee and chocolate until chocolate is melted; cool slightly.

◆ In a large bowl, cream butter or margarine and $^1/_3$ cup of sugar until light and fluffy. Beat in cooled chocolate and egg yolks, then stir in flour.

◆ In a medium bowl, whisk egg whites until stiff, then whisk in remaining sugar. Using a metal spoon, carefully fold whisked egg whites into cake mixture.

◆ Spoon into prepared pan and bake in

preheated oven for 1 to $1^1/_4$ hours, until firm in center. Cool in pan 5 minutes, then turn out carefully onto a wire rack to cool.

◆ Peel paper from cake. Split cake in half horizontally; sandwich together with half of the apricot jam.

◆ In a small pan, heat remaining jam with water; sieve, then brush over top and sides of cake.

♦ To prepare icing, in a small saucepan, gently heat chocolate and half and half, stirring constantly until smooth.

♦ Spread all but 2 tablespoons over top and sides of cake; let stand until set.

♦ In a pastry bag fitted with a writing nozzle, write "Sacher" on cake with reserved icing.

▼ *Spread icing over top and sides of cake.*

Yule Log
Makes 8 servings

Chocolate Cake:

3 eggs

$^1/_2$ cup sugar

$^1/_2$ cup all-purpose flour

$^1/_4$ cup unsweetened cocoa powder

Vanilla Butter Icing:

4 tablespoons unsalted butter, softened

$^3/_4$ cup confectioners' sugar, sifted

2 teaspoons milk

$^1/_2$ teaspoon vanilla extract

To Finish:

1 recipe Chocolate Butter Icing, page 283

Sifted confectioners' sugar

Sprig of holly, if desired

◆ Preheat oven to 400°F. Line a jelly-roll pan with baking parchment and grease the paper.

◆ Prepare sponge cake mixture as for Strawberry Cake, page 229.

♦ Spoon into prepared pan and bake in preheated oven for 8 to 10 minutes, until cake springs back when pressed lightly.

♦ Wring out a clean towel in hot water and place on a flat surface.

♦ Place waxed paper on top and sprinkle with sugar. Turn cake onto paper; peel off lining paper and trim edges.

♦ Roll up cake from a long side, with waxed paper inside. Hold in position a few seconds, then cool on a wire rack with seam underneath.

♦ To prepare vanilla butter icing, in a bowl, beat butter until creamy.

♦ Gradually beat in confectioners' sugar, then milk and vanilla; beat until smooth.

◆ Unroll cake and remove waxed paper. Spread with all but 2 tablespoons of vanilla butter icing and roll up.

◆ Cut a short, diagonal slice off one end and attach to side of roll with chocolate butter icing.

◆ Cover the roll with chocolate butter icing.

◆ Using a palette knife, mark icing to resemble the bark of a tree.

◆ In a pastry bag fitted with a writing nozzle, pipe concentric circles of vanilla icing on ends of log.

◆ Sprinkle with confectioners' sugar to resemble snow and decorate with a holly sprig, if desired.

Chocolate & Chestnut Cake

Makes 8 servings

3 oz. semisweet chocolate, chopped

2 tablespoons water

1 can (15 1/2 oz.) unsweetened chestnut puree

3 eggs, separated

1/2 cup sugar

Filling:

2/3 cup whipping cream

2 tablespoons Cointreau

1 tablespoon honey

1 to 2 tablespoons milk, if needed

To Finish:

2 tablespoons grated semisweet chocolate

2/3 cup whipping cream

◆ Preheat oven to 350°F. Grease a jelly-roll pan and line with baking parchment.

◆ In a small saucepan, gently heat chocolate and water, stirring occasionally until chocolate is melted.

◆ In a blender or food processor fitted with a metal blade, process melted chocolate and half of the chestnut puree until smooth; set aside.

◆ In a large bowl, whisk egg yolks and sugar until thick and creamy, then gradually whisk in chocolate mixture.

◆ In a small bowl, whisk egg whites until fairly stiff. Using a large metal spoon, carefully fold into chocolate mixture.

◆ Spoon into pan and bake 25 to 30 minutes, until firm; cool.

◆ To prepare filling, in a bowl, whip cream until thick.

◆ In food processor, blend remaining chestnut puree with Cointreau and honey until smooth.

◆ Fold into whipped cream, adding milk to thin, if needed.

♦ Turn cake out of pan and cut into three equal strips.

♦ Using three fourths of the filling, carefully sandwich strips together.

♦ Spread remaining filling over sides of cake and coat with most of the chocolate.

♦ In a small bowl, whip whipping cream until thick.

♦ Using a pastry bag fitted with a star nozzle, pipe diagonal lines of whipped cream on top of cake.

♦ Sprinkle remaining grated chocolate between lines.

 *Chocolate*

Sicilian Cassata
Makes 8 servings

Cake:

1 1/2 cups self-rising flour

1 teaspoon baking powder

12 tablespoons margarine, softened

3/4 cup sugar

3 eggs

Filling:

2 cups ricotta cheese

3 1/2 oz. semisweet chocolate, grated

1/2 cup sugar

1 teaspoon vanilla extract

2 tablespoons brandy

1/2 cup chopped candied fruit

1/4 cup chopped almonds

To Decorate:

Sifted confectioners' sugar

Chocolate curls, page 31

♦ Preheat oven to 375°F. Grease a deep, 8-inch round cake pan; line with baking parchment.

♦ To prepare cake, sift flour and baking powder into a large bowl.

♦ Add margarine, sugar, and eggs and beat until smooth and creamy.

♦ Pour into prepared pan and bake in preheated oven 30 to 40 minutes, until golden brown and firm.

♦ Turn out onto a wire rack to cool.

♦ Wash and dry cake pan. Grease and line again.

♦ To prepare filling, sieve ricotta cheese into a medium bowl.

♦ Add chocolate, sugar, vanilla, and brandy; beat thoroughly until mixture is light and fluffy.

♦ Stir in candied fruit and chopped almonds.

◆ Cut thin crust off top of cake and discard. Cut cake horizontally in three slices.

◆ Place one slice in prepared pan. Cover with half of cheese mixture. Repeat layers, finishing with cake.

◆ Press down lightly, cover with a weight, and chill overnight.

◆ To serve, turn cake out onto serving plate. Sprinkle with confectioners' sugar and decorate with chocolate curls.

Striped Chocolate Cake
Makes 8 servings

Chocolate Ganache:

1 1/4 cups whipping cream

10 oz. semisweet chocolate, chopped

Chocolate Cake:

4 eggs

1/2 cup sugar

4 oz. semisweet chocolate, melted, page 22

1/4 cup all-purpose flour

Roulade:

2 eggs plus 1 yolk

1/3 cup sugar

1/2 cup all-purpose flour, sifted

To Decorate:

Chocolate caraque, page 32

Sifted confectioners' sugar

◆ Preheat oven to 350°F.

◆ Grease a deep, 8-inch round cake pan and a jelly-roll pan and line with baking parchment.

◆ To prepare ganache, heat whipping cream until almost boiling. Add chocolate and stir until melted; cool.

◆ To prepare cake, whisk 1 egg, 3 yolks, and sugar. Whisk in chocolate; sift and fold in flour. Whisk egg whites until soft peaks form.

◆ Stir 1 tablespoon into chocolate mixture, then fold in remaining egg whites.

◆ Spoon into pan. Bake 20 to 25 minutes, until just firm in center; cool. Increase heat to 425°F.

◆ To prepare roulade, whisk eggs, yolk, and sugar until pale and thick; fold in flour.

◆ Pour into jelly-roll pan and bake in

preheated oven for 6 minutes or until risen and golden.

♦ Let stand 1 minute; turn out onto waxed paper dredged with confectioners' sugar. Roll up, enclosing paper; cool.

♦ Whisk cooled ganache until light and fluffy.

♦ Turn out cake and cut in half.

♦ Unroll roulade, remove paper, and spread with ganache. Cut in seven 1-in.-wide strips. Roll up, joining strips to form a large roll.

♦ Spread one cake with ganache. Lay roulade on top. Spread thin layer of ganache on the other cake; place on top of roulade. Spread remaining ganache over cake.

♦ Decorate with caraque and confectioners' sugar.

Chocolate Roulade
Makes 6 to 8 servings

Roulade:

4 eggs, separated

$^1/_2$ cup sugar

4 oz. semisweet chocolate, melted, then cooled

Filling:

1 cup whipping cream

5 oz. white chocolate

To Decorate:

Sifted confectioners' sugar

Chocolate rose leaves, page 32

◆ Preheat oven to 350°F. Line a jelly-roll pan with baking parchment.

◆ To prepare roulade, in a medium bowl, whisk egg yolks and sugar until thick and pale.

◆ Gently fold in cooled chocolate.

◆ In small bowl, whisk egg whites until stiff.

♦ Carefully fold into chocolate mixture. Pour into prepared pan and bake in preheated oven for 20 to 25 minutes, until firm.

♦ Cover with a clean towel and leave in pan overnight.

♦ To prepare filling, in a small saucepan, heat whipping cream to just below boiling point.

♦ In a food processor fitted with a metal blade, process white chocolate until chopped.

♦ With motor running, pour hot cream through feed tube. Process 10 to 15 seconds, until mixture is smooth.

♦ Transfer to a medium bowl, cover with plastic wrap, and chill overnight.

♦ Whisk filling until it starts to form soft peaks.

◆ Sprinkle foil with confectioners' sugar. Turn out roulade onto paper. Peel away paper.

◆ Spread filling over roulade and roll up, starting at a short side.

◆ Place on a serving dish. Chill 2 to 3 hours.

◆ Slice and decorate with chocolate rose leaves before serving.

▼ *Roll up, starting at short side.*

Chocolate

Chocolate Truffle Cake
Makes 10 servings

Cake:
1/4 cup sugar

2 eggs

1/4 cup all-purpose flour

1/4 cup unsweetened cocoa powder

1/4 cup cold, strong coffee

1 tablespoon brandy

Truffle Filling:
2 1/2 cups whipping cream

15 oz. semisweet chocolate, melted, then cooled

To Decorate:
Unsweetened cocoa powder

Confectioners' sugar

Chocolate shapes, page 34

◆ Preheat oven to 425°F. Grease a 9-inch springform cake pan and line with baking parchment.

◆ To prepare cake, in a medium bowl set over a pan of hot water, whisk sugar and eggs until pale and thick.

◆ Sift in flour and cocoa; fold gently into mixture.

◆ Pour into prepared pan and bake in preheated oven for 7 to 10 minutes or until firm to the touch.

◆ Transfer to a wire rack to cool. Wash and dry pan. Replace cake in pan when cold.

◆ In a small bowl, mix coffee and brandy; brush over cake.

◆ To prepare truffle filling, in a large bowl, whip whipping cream until very soft peaks form; carefully fold in cooled chocolate.

◆ Pour chocolate mixture over cake. Chill until set.

◆ To decorate, sift cocoa over top of cake and remove carefully from pan.

◆ Using strips of waxed paper as a guide, sift bands of confectioners' sugar over cake to create a striped pattern.

◆ Arrange chocolate diamonds around edge. Cut in slices with a hot knife to serve.

Note: It is essential that the whipping cream is only whipped lightly, as it thickens once the chocolate is added.

Chocolate Fudge Cake

Makes 10 to 12 servings

Cake:

2 tablespoons brandy

$^1/_3$ cup raisins

6 tablespoons unsalted butter

3 tablespoons corn syrup

6 oz. semisweet chocolate, chopped

16 graham crackers, crushed

$^1/_3$ cup glacé cherries, halved

$^1/_3$ cup Brazil nuts, coarsely chopped

Grated peel of 1 orange

Topping:

2 oz. semisweet chocolate,
    broken in pieces

2 tablespoons unsalted butter

Brazil nuts

Glacé cherries

♦ In a small bowl, combine brandy and raisins. Let soak several hours or preferably overnight.

♦ Line an 8 x 4-inch loaf pan with plastic wrap.

♦ In a medium saucepan, gently heat butter, corn syrup, and chocolate until chocolate is melted.

♦ Remove from heat. Stir in brandy and raisins, graham cracker crumbs, glacé cherries, Brazil nuts, and grated orange peel.

♦ Spoon mixture into prepared pan. Chill until firm.

♦ Turn out onto a serving plate and remove plastic wrap.

I'd give up chocolate, but I'm no quitter.

◆ To prepare topping, in a small saucepan, melt chocolate and butter, page 22.

◆ Stir until smooth, then spread over sides and top of cake.

◆ Decorate with Brazil nuts and glacé cherries. Chill until topping has set.

◆ Serve cut in thin slices.

Note: This cake is rather rich, so serve in small slices.

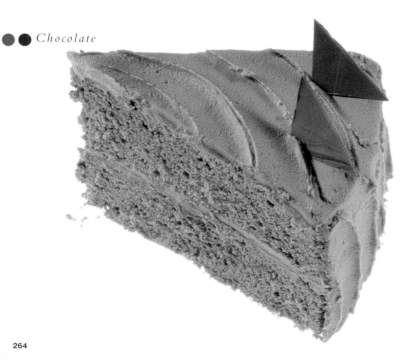

Chocolate

Banana–Chocolate Fudge Cake

Makes 6 to 8 servings

Cake:

12 tablespoons unsalted butter, softened

1¹/₂ cups packed light brown sugar

3 eggs, beaten

3 ripe bananas

2³/₄ cups all-purpose flour

¹/₄ cup unsweetened cocoa powder

1 tablespoon baking powder

3 tablespoons milk

Icing:

2 oz. semisweet chocolate

4 tablespoons unsalted butter

2¹/₃ cups confectioners' sugar

¹/₄ cup half and half

To Decorate:

Chocolate shapes, page 34

♦ Preheat oven to 350°F. Grease two 8-inch round cake pans and line with baking parchment.

♦ To prepare cake, in a large bowl, cream butter and brown sugar until light and fluffy; gradually beat in eggs.

♦ Mash bananas or process in a blender or food processor fitted with a metal blade, until completely smooth.

♦ Stir mashed bananas into brown sugar mixture.

♦ Sift flour, cocoa, and baking powder into a medium bowl.

♦ Gradually stir into creamed mixture alternately with milk to yield a fairly stiff, dropping consistency.

♦ Divide mixture between prepared pans and

bake in preheated oven for about 30 minutes, until well risen and firm to the touch. Turn out onto wire racks to cool.

♦ To prepare icing, in a medium saucepan, melt chocolate and butter, page 22.

♦ Remove from heat and sift in half of the confectioners' sugar; beat until smooth.

♦ Sift in remaining confectioners' sugar.

♦ Stir in half and half and beat well until smooth and thick.

♦ Sandwich cakes together with a fourth of the icing.

♦ Spread remaining icing over top and sides of cake, swirling to make an attractive pattern.

♦ Decorate with chocolate triangles.

Rich Mocha Cake

Makes 8 servings

6 oz. semisweet chocolate, chopped

$^1/_4$ cup cold coffee

12 tablespoons unsalted butter or margarine, softened

1 cup packed dark brown sugar

4 eggs, separated

1$^1/_3$ cups ground almonds

$^1/_2$ cup all-purpose flour, sifted

Coffee Icing:

1$^1/_2$ cups confectioners' sugar

1 tablespoon coffee extract

Water

To Decorate:

8 chocolate-coated nuts, page 43

◆ Preheat oven to 325°F. Grease a deep, 8-inch round cake pan and line with baking parchment.

◆ In a small saucepan, gently heat chocolate and coffee until chocolate is melted; set aside.

◆ In a large bowl, beat butter or margarine and brown sugar until light and fluffy.

◆ Beat in egg yolks, one at a time, then beat in chocolate while still warm.

◆ Fold in ground almonds and flour.

◆ In a medium bowl, whisk egg whites until fairly stiff.

◆ Fold 2 tablespoons of whisked egg whites into chocolate mixture to lighten it, then carefully fold in remaining egg whites.

◆ Spoon into prepared pan and bake in preheated oven for 1 to 1$^{1}/_{4}$ hours or until firm in center. Let stand in pan a few minutes, then turn out onto a wire rack to cool.

◆ To prepare icing, sift confectioners' sugar into a small bowl. Add coffee extract and enough water to mix to a consistency that will coat back of spoon fairly thickly.

◆ Spoon over cake and spread to coat top and sides completely.

◆ Arrange chocolate-coated nuts around edge and let stand until set.

Chocolate

Hazelnut Cake

Makes 8 to 10 servings

3 eggs, 2 separated
¹/₂ cup sugar
¹/₃ cup all-purpose flour
1 tablespoon unsweetened cocoa powder
1 cup hazelnuts, toasted and ground

Chocolate Icing:

1 cup whipping cream
3 oz. semisweet chocolate, chopped

To Finish:

¹/₂ cup chopped hazelnuts, toasted
1 oz. semisweet chocolate,
melted, page 22

♦ Preheat oven to 350°F. Line two 8-inch round cake pans with baking parchment. Grease and flour paper.

♦ In a medium bowl, mix whole egg, 2 yolks, and sugar, using an electric mixer, until thick and mousse-like.

♦ In a small bowl, whisk egg whites until stiff.

♦ Sift flour and cocoa together, then fold into egg mixture with ground nuts. Fold in whisked egg whites.

♦ Spoon into prepared pans and bake in preheated oven 20 to 25 minutes, until cakes spring back when lightly pressed in center. Turn out onto a wire rack to cool.

♦ To prepare chocolate icing, in a small saucepan, very gently heat whipping cream and chocolate, stirring constantly until chocolate is melted. Pour into a small bowl. Cool and then chill.

♦ Whisk icing until thick. Use a third to sandwich the cakes together. Spread more icing around sides and coat with chopped hazelnuts.

♦ Spread remaining icing over top and smooth evenly to the edges. In a pastry bag fitted with a writing nozzle, drizzle melted chocolate over top of cake.

▼ *Coat sides of cake with chopped hazelnuts.*

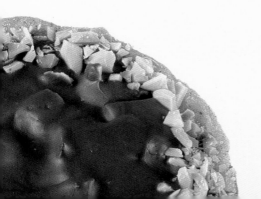

Pastries

Chocolate Rondelles
Makes 8 servings

Cake:
1/3 cup sugar

2 eggs

1/2 cup all-purpose flour, sifted

Chocolate Icing:
1 cup whipping cream

3 oz. semisweet chocolate, chopped

To Finish:
1/4 cup chopped almonds, toasted

1 oz. semisweet chocolate, melted, page 22

◆ Preheat oven to 375°F. Grease and flour two or three baking sheets.

◆ To prepare cake, in a small bowl, beat sugar and eggs, using an electric mixer, until very thick and mousse-like and mixture leaves a trail when beaters are lifted.

◆ Using a metal spoon, carefully fold in flour.

◆ Using a pastry bag fitted with a $1/2$-inch plain nozzle, pipe mixture in twenty-four $2^1/4$-inch circles on prepared baking sheets.

◆ Bake in preheated oven 6 to 8 minutes, until golden brown. Remove with a palette knife and cool on a wire rack.

◆ To prepare icing, in a small saucepan, very gently heat whipping cream and chocolate, stirring costantly, until chocolate is melted.

◆ Refrigerate until cold, then whip until thick. Sandwich three cakes together with some of the icing, then ice the top and sides.

◆ Sprinkle almonds over top. Repeat with remaining cakes, icing, and almonds.

◆ In a pastry bag fitted with a writing nozzle, drizzle chocolate over top of each cake.

"Strength is the capacity to break a chocolate bar into four pieces with your bare hands—and then eat just one of the pieces."
–Judith Viorst

 *Chocolate*

Chocolate Japonais

Makes 8 servings

2 egg whites
$^1/_2$ cup hazelnuts, ground
$^1/_2$ cup sugar

Chocolate Butter Icing:

1 tablespoon unsweetened cocoa powder
1 tablespoon boiling water
6 tablespoons unsalted butter, softened
1 cup confectioners' sugar, sifted

Glacé Icing:

$^3/_4$ cup confectioners' sugar
2 teaspoons unsweetened cocoa powder
2 to 3 teaspoons water

To Finish:

$^1/_4$ cup hazelnuts, toasted and ground
Chocolate rose leaves, page 32

◆ Preheat oven to 300°F. Line two baking sheets with baking parchment.

◆ In a small bowl, whisk egg whites until stiff, then fold in ground hazelnuts and sugar.

◆ Using a pastry bag fitted with a ¹/₂-inch plain nozzle, pipe egg white mixture in sixteen 2-inch circles on the baking sheets.

◆ Bake in preheated oven 50 to 60 minutes; transfer to a wire rack to cool.

◆ To prepare chocolate butter icing, blend cocoa with boiling water; allow to cool.

◆ In a medium bowl, beat butter until creamy. Gradually beat in confectioners' sugar until smooth, then beat in cooled cocoa.

◆ Sandwich rounds together in pairs with some of the icing; spread more around sides. Coat sides of each cake with toasted ground hazelnuts.

◆ To make glacé icing, sift confectioners' sugar and cocoa into a small bowl. Add enough water to make a smooth, thick icing.

◆ Place a spoonful of glacé icing on each cake and spread to the edges. Let stand until set.

◆ Using a pastry bag fitted with a star nozzle, pipe a rosette of remaining chocolate butter icing on each cake and decorate with a chocolate rose leaf.

▼ *Draw circles on each sheet as a guide.*

Chocolatines
Makes 16 servings

Genoise Cake:

3 tablespoons unsalted butter or margarine
3 eggs
¹/₃ cup sugar
³/₄ cup all-purpose flour, sifted

Crème Ganache:

8 oz. semisweet chocolate, chopped
4 tablespoons unsalted butter or margarine
²/₃ cup half and half

To Finish:

³/₄ cup chopped almonds, browned

◆ Preheat oven to 375°F. Grease an 8-inch square pan and line with baking parchment.

◆ To prepare cake, in a small saucepan, very gently heat the butter or margarine until just melted; do not allow it to become hot or oily.

Put "eat chocolate" at the top of your list of things to do today. That way, at least you'll get one thing done.

♦ In a small bowl, beat eggs and sugar using an electric mixer until very thick and mousse-like.

♦ Fold in flour; when nearly incoporated, very carefully fold in butter or margarine as quickly as possible, but be careful not to deflate.

◆ Spoon into prepared pan and bake in preheated oven 30 to 35 minutes, until cake springs back when lightly pressed.

◆ Turn out onto a wire rack to cool.

◆ To prepare crème ganache, in a small saucepan, gently heat chocolate, butter or margarine, and half and half, stirring until melted and smooth.

◆ Cool, then beat well until very smooth.

◆ Split cake in half horizontally and sandwich with some of the ganache. Using a sharp knife, cut cake into sixteen squares.

◆ Spread more ganache on sides of each square and coat with chopped almonds.

◆ In a pastry bag fitted with a fluted nozzle, pipe remaining ganache over top of each cake.

Chamonix
Makes 12 servings

Meringue:
2 egg whites
$^1/_2$ cup sugar

Chestnut Puree:
1 lb. chestnuts
3 oz. semisweet chocolate, chopped
$^1/_4$ cup half and half

Cream Filling:
1 egg white

1 tablespoon sugar
1 cup whipping cream, whipped

To Decorate:
Grated semisweet chocolate

◆ Preheat oven to 250°F. Line two baking sheets with baking parchment.

◆ To prepare meringue, in a small bowl, whisk egg whites until very stiff, then whisk in half

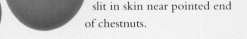

of the sugar. Carefully
fold in remaining sugar.

slit in skin near pointed end
of chestnuts.

♦ Using a pastry bag fitted with a
$1/2$-inch plain nozzle, pipe meringue in twelve
3-inch circles on prepared baking sheets.

♦ Place in a large saucepan, cover with boiling
water, and let stand 2 to 3 minutes.

♦ Bake in preheated oven for $1^1/2$ hours. Cool
on baking sheets.

♦ Remove from water, one at a time, and peel
off both outer and inner skin.

♦ Meanwhile, prepare chestnut puree. Cut a

♦ Return chestnuts to cleaned pan and cover
with a mixture of milk and water.

◆ Cover and simmer for 20 to 30 minutes or until soft. Drain and press through a sieve.

◆ In a small pan, gently heat chocolate and half and half, stirring until chocolate is melted.

◆ Beat in chestnut puree and spoon into a pastry bag fitted with a $1/8$-inch writing nozzle.

◆ To prepare filling, in a bowl, whisk egg white until stiff, then whisk in sugar.

◆ Fold in whipping cream and set aside.

◆ Remove meringues from baking sheets and pipe chestnut puree around top edge of each to form a nest.

◆ Fill center with cream filling and sprinkle with grated chocolate.

Ginger & Chocolate Meringues
Makes 8 servings

4 egg whites

1¼ cups sugar

4 oz. semisweet chocolate, grated

Filling:

1¼ cups whipping cream

3 pieces Chinese stem ginger, finely chopped

1 tablespoon syrup from Chinese stem ginger

½ teaspoon ground cinnamon

To Decorate:

Chocolate leaves, page 32

◆ Preheat oven to 250°F. Line two baking sheets with baking parchment.

◆ In a medium bowl, whisk egg whites until stiff.

◆ Whisk in half of the sugar.

295

◆ Fold in remaining sugar with grated chocolate.

◆ Pipe or spoon sixteen tablespoonfuls of meringue mixture onto prepared baking sheets, allowing room to spread slightly.

◆ Bake in preheated oven for $1^1/2$ hours or until dry. Transfer to wire racks to cool.

◆ To prepare filling, in a small bowl, whip whipping cream until thick.

◆ Stir in ginger syrup, then add chopped ginger and cinnamon.

◆ Use filling to sandwich meringues together.

◆ Decorate with chocolate leaves to serve.

Variations: Omit grated chocolate from meringue mixture. When meringues are cooked, melt 4 oz. semisweet chocolate. Dip bottom of each cooled meringue shell into melted chocolate. Let set on waxed paper. Sandwich together with ginger cream.

Alternatively, pipe meringues in fingers using a pastry bag fitted with a ³/₄-inch plain or fluted nozzle. Dip ends of meringues into melted chocolate when cool. Let set on waxed paper. Sandwich together with ginger cream.

▼ *Leave room for each meringue to spread.*

Chocolate Cream Drops

Makes 20 pieces

Drops:

3 eggs

½ cup sugar

¾ cup plus 2 tablespoons all-purpose flour

2 tablespoons unsweetened cocoa powder

Chocolate Ganache:

1 cup whipping cream

8 oz. semisweet chocolate, chopped

To Decorate:

2 oz. white chocolate, melted, page 22

◆ Preheat oven to 375°F. Grease four baking sheets and line with baking parchment.

◆ To prepare drops, in a medium bowl, whisk eggs and sugar until the mixture is thick and light and the whisk leaves a trial when lifted.

◆ Sift flour and cocoa onto mixture; fold in gently.

◆ Drop teaspoonfuls of mixture onto prepared baking sheets, leaving a 2-inch space between each spoonful.

◆ Bake in preheated oven, in two batches, for 10 minutes or until firm.

◆ Let stand on baking sheets a few minutes, then transfer to wire racks to cool.

◆ To prepare chocolate ganache, in a medium saucepan, heat whipping cream until almost boiling.

◆ Remove from heat and add chocolate; stir until smooth.

Chocolate is nature's way of making up for Mondays.

♦ Cool, then whisk until thick and light.

♦ Sandwich drops together with ganache.

♦ To decorate, using a pastry bag fitted with a writing nozzle, drizzle white chocolate over top of each drop.

Note: Chocolate cream drops are at their best about 2 hours after filling.

Variations: Drizzle with semisweet chocolate rather than white chocolate, or dust drops with sifted confectioners' sugar.

Barcettos

Makes 12 servings

Almond Pastry:

$^1/_2$ cup all-purpose flour

$^1/_4$ cup ground almonds

2 tablespoons unsalted butter, softened

2 tablespoons sugar

1 egg yolk

1 teaspoon water

Frangipane:

$^1/_4$ cup sugar

$^1/_3$ cup ground almonds

1 egg white

Few drops of almond extract

To Finish:

1 oz. semisweet chocolate, melted, page 22

◆ Preheat oven to 375°F.

◆ To prepare pastry, sift flour onto a cool work surface and sprinkle with ground almonds.

◆ Make a well in center and add butter, sugar, egg yolk, and water.

◆ Using fingertips of one hand, work these ingredients together, then draw in flour and almonds.

◆ Knead lightly until smooth; wrap in plastic wrap and chill for 1 hour.

◆ On a lightly floured surface, roll out pastry thinly and line twelve 3-inch barquette molds.

◆ Prick bottoms and chill for 15 minutes.

◆ To prepare frangipane, combine all ingredients in a small bowl and mix thoroughly.

◆ Divide mixture among molds, place on a baking sheet, and bake in preheated oven for 12 to 15 minutes.

♦ Transfer to a wire rack to cool.

♦ In a pastry bag fitted with a writing nozzle, drizzle chocolate on top of each barquette.

Note: Almond pastry should be rolled very thinly.

Chocolate Almond Tartlets
Makes 10 servings

Pâte Sucrée:
¹/₂ cup all-purpose flour
2 tablespoons unsalted butter, softened
2 tablespoons sugar
1 egg yolk

Filling:
¹/₃ cup packed dark brown sugar
2 tablespoons corn syrup
4 tablespoons unsalted butter
1 tablespoon water

1 cup slivered almonds, chopped and toasted
2 oz. semisweet chocolate, melted, page 22

◆ Preheat oven to 375°F.

◆ To prepare pâte sucrée, sift flour onto a cool work surface. Make a well in center and add butter, sugar, and egg yolk.

◆ Using fingertips of one hand, work these ingredients together, then draw in flour.

◆ Knead lightly until smooth, then chill 1 hour.

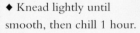

◆ On a lightly floured surface, roll out pastry very thinly and line twelve tartlet molds.

◆ Prick bottoms and chill for 15 minutes.

◆ Press a square of foil into each tartlet and bake blind for 8 to 10 minutes, until golden.

◆ Remove foil and cool on a wire rack.

◆ To prepare filling, combine brown sugar, corn syrup, butter, and water in a small, heavy-bottomed saucepan.

◆ Heat gently, stirring constantly, until sugar is dissolved.

◆ Boil 5 to 7 minutes at 240°F or until a small

Man cannot live by chocolate alone—but woman can!

amount of mixture forms a soft ball when dropped into cold water.

◆ Stir in all but 1 tablespoon of the almonds. Spoon filling into pastry cups before it begins to set.

◆ Chop reserved almonds finely. Spread melted chocolate over filling and sprinkle chopped nuts around edge of each tartlet.

Note: Pâte sucrée should be rolled very thinly.

Strawberry-Chocolate Tarts

Makes 4 servings

Pastry:

7 tablespoons butter, softened

2 teaspoons confectioners' sugar

1 egg yolk

1 tablespoon water

1 1/2 cups all-purpose flour

Chocolate Filling:

4 tablespoons unsalted butter, softened

1/4 cup sugar

1 egg, beaten

2 oz. semisweet chocolate, grated

1/2 cup ground almonds

Topping:

1 tablespoon plus 1 teaspoon red currant jelly

1 teaspoon kirsch

8 oz. strawberries, hulled and halved

◆ To prepare pastry, in a medium bowl, cream butter and confectioners' sugar until soft and light.

♦ In a small bowl, mix egg yolk and water; gradually stir into creamed mixture.

♦ Sift flour into mixture and mix to a smooth dough with a round-bladed knife. Wrap in plastic wrap and chill for 1 hour.

♦ Preheat oven to 375°F.

♦ On a lightly floured surface, roll out pastry thinly and line four 4-inch quiche pans.

♦ To prepare filling, in a small bowl, beat butter and sugar until creamy, then beat in egg.

♦ Stir in chocolate; add ground almonds and mix to a soft, dropping consistency.

♦ Divide among pastry shells.

♦ Bake in preheated oven 20 to 25 minutes, until filling is set and pastry is crisp.

♦ To prepare topping, in a small saucepan, gently heat red currant jelly, stirring until completely dissolved.

♦ Stir in kirsch. Brush over chocolate tarts while still warm.

♦ Arrange strawberry halves on top and brush with remaining red currant jelly.

♦ Transfer to a wire rack to cool.

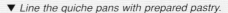

▼ *Line the quiche pans with prepared pastry.*

Chocolate Pastry Tartlets
Makes 12 servings

Pastry:
³/4 cup plus 2 tablespoons all-purpose flour
2 tablespoons unsweetened cocoa powder
4 tablespoons butter, softened
2 tablespoons confectioners' sugar, sifted
1 egg yolk
Pinch of salt

Filling:
¹/3 cup whipping cream
1 cup strawberry fromage frais, see page 317

1 teaspoon triple-strength rose water
6 oz. red currants

To Decorate:
Frosted leaves, if desired

◆ Preheat oven to 350°F.

◆ To prepare pastry, sift flour and cocoa into a large bowl.

♦ Add butter, confectioners' sugar, egg yolk, and salt.

♦ Work ingredients together with fingers until mixture forms a firm dough.

♦ Wrap in plastic wrap and chill 30 minutes, until firm.

♦ On a floured surface, roll out pastry thinly and line twelve tartlet pans; prick bottoms.

♦ Press a piece of foil into each tartlet.

♦ Bake in preheated oven 10 minutes. Remove foil and bake 10 minutes more or until pastry is golden and firm to the touch.

♦ Transfer to a wire rack to cool.

♦ In a medium bowl, whip whipping cream lightly. Fold in fromage frais and rose water.

♦ Place a spoonful of filling in each tartlet and arrange red currants on top.

♦ Decorate with frosted leaves, if desired. Serve as soon as possible.

Note: If strawberry-flavored fromage frais is unobtainable, use crème fraíche or plain fromage frais.

▼ *Line tartlet pans and press foil into each.*

Pains au Chocolat
Makes 8 servings

2 cups bread flour

1 teaspoon salt

2 teaspoons fast-rising yeast

3/4 cup milk

1 tablespoon plus 2 teaspoons sugar

1 tablespoon vegetable oil

7 tablespoons butter

1/2 cup semisweet chocolate pieces (3 oz.)

Glaze:

1 egg yolk

1 tablespoon plus 1 teaspoon milk

◆ Sift flour and salt into a large bowl. Stir in yeast. Make well in center.

◆ In a small saucepan, heat milk to 120°F to 130°F. Add sugar and oil; stir until sugar is dissolved. Add to flour; mix well. Knead lightly on floured surface until smooth.

◆ Place dough in cleaned bowl; cover and let

rise in a warm place 1 to 2 hours, until tripled in size.

◆ Knead again, return to bowl, cover, and let rise again 1 to 2 hours or until doubled in size. Knead, then roll in a rectangle three times as long as it is wide.

◆ Divide butter into thirds. Dot one portion in small pieces over top two thirds of dough, leaving a $1/2$-inch border. Fold lower third up and top third down; press edges with rolling pin to seal.

◆ Give dough a half-turn and roll in a rectangle as before. Repeat process twice with remaining butter. Then fold dough in half, place in an oiled bowl, cover, and chill 1 hour.

◆ Cut dough in half; roll out each half to a 12 x 6-inch rectangle. Cut into four 6 x 3-inch rectangles.

♦ Sprinkle a line of chocolate pieces along short end of each rectangle. Roll up, jelly-roll style. Place rolls seam-side down on a buttered baking sheet and let stand in a warm place until doubled in size.

♦ Preheat oven to 425°F.

♦ In a small bowl, mix egg yolk and milk; brush over rolls. Bake in center of oven for 15 to 20 minutes, until well risen.

▼ *Knead dough firmly with the ball of the hand.*

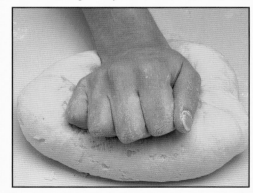

Walnut & Chocolate Fingers

Makes 24 pieces

5 sheets phyllo pastry
4 tablespoons unsalted butter, melted

Filling:

1 1/4 cups walnut pieces, coarsely ground
2 tablespoons sugar
1/2 teaspoon ground cinnamon
2 oz. semisweet chocolate, grated

To Decorate:

1 tablespoon confectioners' sugar

◆ Preheat oven to 325°F. Grease two baking sheets.

◆ To prepare filling, in a small bowl, mix ground walnuts, sugar, cinnamon, and grated chocolate.

◆ Cut each sheet of phyllo pastry into four 9 x 7-inch rectangles.

◆ Pile on top of each other and cover with a

towel to keep the pastry from drying out.

◆ Brush a phyllo rectangle with melted butter.

◆ Spread 1 teaspoon of filling along one short end. Fold long sides in, slightly overfilling. Roll up from filling end.

◆ Place on prepared baking sheet with seam underneath; brush with melted butter.

◆ Repeat with remaining pastry and filling.

◆ Bake in preheated oven for 20 minutes or until very lightly browned.

◆ Transfer to a wire rack to cool. Dust with sifted confectioners' sugar to serve.

Variations:
Almond Fingers: Substitute ground almonds

for walnuts and orange flower water for cinnamon.

Pistachio Fingers: Substitute finely chopped pistachios for walnuts and rose water for cinnamon.

Pine Nut Fingers: Substitute finely chopped pine nuts for walnuts and orange flower water for cinnamon.

▼ *Cover with towel to keep pastry moist.*

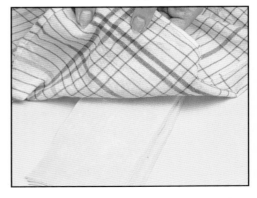

Cookies & Bars

Chocolate Checkerboards
Makes 48 cookies

3/4 cup butter, softened

3/4 cup sugar

1 teaspoon vanilla extract

2 eggs

4 1/2 cups all-purpose flour

2 teaspoons baking powder

1 teaspoon milk

2 tablespoons unsweetened cocoa powder

◆ Preheat oven to 350°F.

◆ Grease several baking sheets.

◆ Divide butter and sugar equally between two bowls.

◆ To make vanilla dough, beat half of the butter and sugar until light and fluffy.

◆ Beat in vanilla and 1 egg.

◆ In another bowl, sift half of the flour and 1 teaspoon baking powder.

◆ Blend in with spoon, then work by hand to form a smooth dough.

◆ Make chocolate dough in same way with remaining ingredients, adding milk with egg and sifting cocoa powder in with flour.

◆ Divide each portion into four equal pieces.

◆ On a floured surface, roll each piece of dough into a rope 12 inches long.

◆ Place one chocolate rope next to a vanilla rope. Place a chocolate on top of the vanilla and a vanilla on top of the chocolate.

◆ Press firmly together to form a square. Wrap in plastic wrap.

◆ Repeat with remaining dough.

◆ Refrigerate for 1 hour.

◆ Cut dough into forty-eight slices and place on the baking sheets.

◆ Bake 20 minutes, until lightly browned.

◆ Cool on wire racks.

▼ *Press ropes firmly together.*

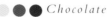

Florentines

Makes about 28 pieces

¹/4 cup unsalted butter

¹/3 cup whipping cream

¹/3 cup sugar

Finely shredded zest of 1 lemon

1 teaspoon lemon juice

¹/2 cup all-purpose flour, sifted

¹/2 cup slivered blanched almonds

³/4 cup chopped mixed candied citrus peel

¹/3 cup chopped candied cherries

2 tablespoons golden raisins

2 tablespoons chopped angelica

To Finish:

3 oz. semisweet chocolate, chopped

3 oz. white chocolate, chopped

◆ Preheat oven to 350°F. Grease several baking sheets and line with baking parchment.

◆ Put butter, cream, sugar, lemon zest, and juice into a medium saucepan.

◆ Stir over a medium heat until butter melts. ◆

Remove from heat and stir in flour, almonds, mixed peel, cherries, golden raisins, and angelica.

◆ Drop teaspoonfuls of mixture onto prepared baking sheets, spacing well apart.

◆ Using a fork dipped in cold water, flatten each mound to a circle about $2^1/_2$ inches in diameter.

◆ Bake 10 to 12 minutes, until lightly browned around the edges.

◆ Cool on baking sheets a few minutes, then remove with a spatula to wire racks to cool completely.

◆ Melt semisweet and white chocolate separately in two heatproof bowls placed over pans of simmering water.

♦ Spread flat sides of half the florentines with semisweet chocolate and the remaning florentines with white chocolate.

♦ Using a fork, mark chocolate into wavy lines.

♦ Leave to set, chocolate sides up.

▼ *Mark chocolate in wavy lines with a fork.*

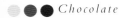

Almond Fingers

Makes about 15 pieces

1 egg white
1¹/₄ cups ground almonds
2 tablespoons ground rice
²/₃ cup sugar
Rice paper
1 oz. semisweet chocolate, melted, page 22

◆ Preheat oven to 325°F. In a medium bowl, lightly whisk egg white, then add ground almonds, ground rice, and sugar.

◆ Mix to a firm consistency, then divide into four pieces.

◆ Roll each piece in a sausage shape about 16 inches long. Arrange close together so that long sides are touching, forming a four-fold long strip.

◆ Cut strip diagonally in 1¹/₄-inch widths.

◆ Lift each piece onto rice paper, spacing a

little apart to allow for spreading, and place
on a baking sheet.

◆ Bake in preheated oven 20 minutes, until
golden brown, then transfer to a wire rack
to cool. Tear off any excess rice paper.

◆ In a pastry bag fitted with a writing nozzle,
drizzle chocolate over fingers.

337

Hazlenut-Chocolate Crescents

Makes 40 pieces

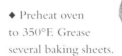

16 tablespoons unsalted butter, softened

^{1}/$_3$ cup sugar

1 egg yolk

1 teaspoon rum

2 cups blanched hazelnuts, ground

2 cups all-purpose flour

^{1}/$_2$ cup cornstarch

2 tablespoons unsweetened cocoa powder

To Decorate:

^{1}/$_3$ cup confectioners' sugar, sifted

◆ Preheat oven to 350°F. Grease several baking sheets.

◆ In a large bowl, cream butter and sugar until pale and fluffy.

◆ Beat in egg yolk and rum. Stir in ground hazelnuts.

◆ Sift 2 cups flour, cornstarch, and cocoa

Chocolate is an aphrodisiac—
it increases the desire for
more chocolate.

together over mixture. Stir in dry ingredients, adding a little more flour if necessary to make a firm dough.

◆ With lightly floured hands, break off walnut-sized pieces of dough.

♦ Roll each in a 3-inch length, tapering in pointed ends. Shape into crescents and place on prepared baking sheets.

♦ Bake in preheated oven 20 to 25 minutes, until firm.

♦ Transfer to wire racks to cool.

♦ Gently toss crescents in confectioners' sugar to coat completely.

Note: If possible, grind hazelnuts in a food processor fitted with a metal blade or in a blender. Do not use ready-ground hazelnuts, as they are too fine.

Variation: Freshly ground almonds or walnuts may be used instead of hazelnuts.

Chocolate

Almond & Chocolate Tuiles

Makes 18 pieces

4 tablespoons unsalted butter

2 egg whites

$^1/_2$ cup sugar

$^1/_3$ cup all-purpose flour

2 tablespoons unsweetened cocoa powder

$^1/_4$ cup sliced almonds

Grated peel of 1 orange

◆ Preheat oven to 350°F. Grease two or three baking sheets and a rolling pin.

◆ In a small saucepan, melt butter and cool.

◆ In a small bowl, using a fork, whisk egg whites and sugar until mixture is frothy.

◆ Sift flour and cocoa into egg whites.

◆ Add sliced almonds and orange peel; mix with a fork.

◆ Add cooled butter and mix thoroughly.

♦ Drop teaspoonfuls of mixture onto prepared baking sheets, leaving 5 inches of space between each.

♦ Using a palette knife, spread each spoonful of mixture out slightly.

♦ Bake in preheated oven, one sheet at a time, for 8 to 10 minutes, until edges feel firm.

♦ Lift cookies off sheets carefully with a palette knife and place on a rolling pin while still warm.

♦ Let set 2 minutes, until set in a curved shape; transfer to a wire rack to cool completely. Store in an airtight container.

Variations: To make tulip-shaped baskets for serving ice cream, shape cooked tuiles over small, greased bowls or glasses.

A single cup of coffee
contains the same amount
of caffeine as an entire pound
of chocolate.

Double Chocolate Cookies

Makes about 48 cookies

$^1/_2$ cup butter

$^1/_4$ cup sugar

$^1/_3$ cup packed brown sugar

1 egg, beaten

$^1/_2$ teaspoon vanilla extract

1 cup plus 2 tablespoons all-purpose flour

2 tablespoons unsweetened cocoa powder

$^1/_2$ teaspoon baking soda

5 oz. white chocolate, cut into pieces

◆ Preheat oven to 350°F.

◆ Butter several baking sheets.

◆ In a bowl, beat butter with sugars until creamy.

◆ Gradually beat in egg and vanilla extract.

◆ Into another bowl, sift flour, cocoa powder, and baking soda.

◆ Mix well, then stir in chocolate pieces.

347

◆ Drop teaspoonfuls of dough, spaced well apart, onto prepared baking sheets.

◆ Bake 10 to 12 minutes, until firm.

◆ Cool on baking sheets a few minutes, then remove to wire racks to cool completely.

Variations:

Vanilla Chocolate Chip Cookies: Omit cocoa and add an extra 2 tablespoons flour.

Mocha Chocolate Chip Cookies: Add 2 teaspoons instant coffee granules with flour and cocoa.

Fruit & Chocolate Chip Cookies: Replace nuts with $1/3$ cup each chopped dried apricots and pineapple and coconut flakes.

▼ *Stir in white chocolate pieces.*

▼ *Drop teaspoonfuls of dough onto baking sheets.*

Chocolate Muffins
Makes 12 muffins

$2^1/_4$ cups all-purpose flour

1 tablespoon baking powder

$^1/_2$ teaspoon salt

1 tablespoon plus 2 teaspoons sugar

$^1/_4$ cup semisweet chocolate pieces (2 oz.)

4 tablespoons butter, melted, then cooled

1 egg, beaten

1 cup milk

Orange Butter:

8 tablespoons unsalted butter, softened

2 tablespoons confectioners' sugar

2 tablespoons fresh orange juice

Grated peel of $^1/_2$ orange

◆ Preheat oven to 400°F. Thoroughly grease a deep, 12-cup muffin pan or line with paper baking cups.

◆ Sift flour, baking powder, and salt into a large bowl.

◆ Stir in sugar and chocolate pieces.

◆ In a small bowl, mix cooled butter, egg, and milk.

◆ Pour into dry ingredients and stir until flour is just moistened but looks lumpy.

◆ Spoon mixture into prepared cups.

◆ Bake in preheated oven 15 to 20 minutes, until well risen and golden brown.

◆ Cool in cups 5 minutes before serving.

◆ To prepare orange butter, in a small bowl, beat all ingredients until light and fluffy.

◆ Serve muffins warm with orange butter.

Note: If serving muffins for breakfast, mix dry ingredients in a bowl and make orange butter the day before. It takes only a matter of minutes to stir in liquid and bake the muffins the next morning.

Lebkuchen
Makes 24 pieces

Rice paper

3 eggs

1 cup sugar

1 cup all-purpose flour

1 teaspoon ground cinnamon

$^1/_4$ teaspoon ground cloves

$^1/_4$ teaspoon grated nutmeg

$^1/_2$ teaspoon ground cardamom

$1^3/_4$ cups unblanched almonds, coarsely ground

2 tablespoons candied lemon peel, finely chopped

2 tablespoons candied orange peel, finely chopped

$1^1/_2$ oz. semisweet chocolate, grated

$^1/_2$ teaspoon grated lemon peel

$^1/_2$ teaspoon grated orange peel

2 teaspoons triple-strength rose water

Icing:

1 egg white

2 teaspoons unsweetened cocoa powder blended with
 1 tablespoon boiling water

$^3/_4$ cup confectioners' sugar

2 tablespoons sugar crystals

◆ Preheat oven to 325°F. Line bottom of a jelly-roll pan with rice paper.

◆ In a large bowl, whisk eggs and sugar until mixture is thick and light and the whisk leaves a trail when lifted.

◆ Sift in flour and spices.

◆ Stir in almonds, candied citrus peels, grated chocolate, and grated lemon and orange peels.

◆ Spread mixture evenly in prepared pan and brush with rose water.

◆ Bake in preheated oven 30 to 35 minutes, until firm.

◆ To prepare icing, in a small bowl, stir egg white into cooled cocoa.

◆ Sift in confectioners' sugar and mix thoroughly. Spread icing on cake while warm.

"I never met a chocolate
I didn't like."
-Deanna Troi, *Star Trek: The
Next Generation*

◆ Sprinkle with sugar crystals and return to
oven for about 5 minutes. Cut into squares
when cooled.

Panforte di Siena

Makes 12 to 16 servings

¹/₃ cup glacé cherries, quartered
¹/₃ cup candied orange peel, finely chopped
¹/₃ cup candied lemon peel, finely chopped
2 tablespoons crystallized ginger, coarsely chopped
³/₄ cup sliced almonds
³/₄ cup hazelnuts, toasted and coarsely ground
¹/₂ cup all-purpose flour
¹/₄ cup unsweetened cocoa powder
1 teaspoon ground cinnamon
¹/₄ teaspoon ground cloves
¹/₃ cup honey

¹/₂ cup sugar
1 teaspoon orange flower water

To Decorate:
Confectioners' sugar

◆ Preheat oven to 325°F. Thoroughly grease bottom of an 8-inch, loose-bottomed cake or flan pan. Line bottom with waxed paper; grease again.

◆ In a medium bowl, mix glacé cherries, orange and lemon peels, ginger, almonds, and hazelnuts.

◆ Sift in flour, cocoa, cinnamon, and cloves and mix thoroughly; set aside.

◆ In a medium saucepan, heat honey, sugar, and orange flower water until sugar is dissolved.

◆ Bring to a boil and boil steadily until mixture reaches soft ball stage (around 240°F).

◆ To test, drop a small amount of syrup into a cup of cold water; it should form a soft ball.

◆ Quickly remove pan from heat, stir in prepared dry ingredients, and mix thoroughly.

◆ Spoon into prepared pan, spread evenly, and bake in preheated oven for 30 minutes.

◆ Cool in pan.

◆ Turn out and peel away waxed paper.

◆ Sift confectioners' sugar over top and cut into wedges to serve.

Sweets & Drinks

Chocolate

Cream Truffles

Makes 20 pieces

¹/₃ cup whipping cream

1 vanilla bean

1 tablespoon plus 2 teaspoons sugar

1 egg yolk

5 oz. semisweet chocolate, chopped

2 tablespoons unsalted butter

2 teaspoons crème de cacao

Coating:

1 tablespoon plus 1 teaspoon unsweetened cocoa powder

2 teaspoons confectioners' sugar

◆ Line a jelly-roll pan with baking parchment.

◆ In a medium saucepan, bring whipping cream and vanilla bean almost to a boil.

◆ Remove from heat, cover, and set aside for 30 minutes. Remove vanilla bean.

◆ In a small bowl, whisk sugar and egg yolk until pale and thick; whisk into whipping cream.

◆ Return pan to heat and gently heat without boiling.

◆ Add chocolate and butter, stirring until mixture is smooth.

◆ Stir in crème de cacao.

◆ Pour into prepared pan and chill 1 hour or until firm.

◆ To prepare coating, sift cocoa and confectioners' sugar onto a plate.

◆ Pull off small pieces of chilled truffle mixture and roll in balls.

◆ Roll each ball in sifted cocoa mixture and place in paper cups, if desired.

To keep chocolate from melting, eat it faster.

♦ Refrigerate and eat within three days.

Variations: Use brandy, rum, or another liqueur instead of crème de cacao.

Truffles may be coated in melted semisweet or white chocolate, or rolled in crushed praline or nuts, as an alternative to cocoa and confectioners' sugar. Drizzled contrasting chocolate makes an attractive finish for chocolate-coated truffles.

Chocolate

Collettes
Makes 20 pieces

9 oz. semisweet chocolate
¹/₂ teaspoon sunflower oil
²/₃ cup whipping cream
Finely grated peel of ¹/₂ orange
1 tablespoon Cointreau

To Decorate:
Blanched almonds
Chopped nuts
Chocolate-coated nuts, page 43

◆ In a small saucepan, melt 5 oz. of chocolate with oil.

◆ Using double petit four paper cups, brush chocolate evenly over the insides of twenty cups. Chill until set. Apply a second coat of chocolate, remelting if necessary. Chill until completely set.

◆ In a small saucepan, heat whipping cream with grated orange peel until boiling.

369

◆ Remove from heat, add remaining chocolate, and stir until smooth. Return pan to heat and stir until mixture begins to bubble. Gradually stir in Cointreau; cool.

◆ Peel paper cups off chocolate cups.

◆ Beat cooled chocolate cream until thick. In a pastry bag fitted with a fluted nozzle, pipe cream into chocolate cups.

◆ Decorate with whole, chopped, and chocolate-coated nuts. Refrigerate and eat within two or three days.

Variations: Use a small amount of coffee extract, praline powder, or finely chopped nuts in place of grated orange peel.

Use an alternative liqueur, such as rum or brandy, instead of Cointreau.

Use white chocolate in filling instead of semisweet chocolate.

▼ *Brush chocolate evenly over insides of cups.*

▼ *Pipe chocolate cream into chocolate cups.*

Chocolate Nut Fudge
Makes 1¹/2 pounds

8 tablespoons unsalted butter

¹/4 cup coffee

2 tablespoons unsweetened cocoa powder

2 tablespoons corn syrup

3 cups sugar

³/4 cup plus 2 tablespoons sweetened condensed milk

1 cup chopped pecans

◆ Grease an 11 x 7-inch baking pan.

◆ In a large saucepan, combine butter, coffee, cocoa, corn syrup, and sugar.

◆ Heat gently, stirring occasionally, until sugar is dissolved; do not allow to boil at this stage or finished fudge will crystallize and will not have a smooth texture.

◆ Add condensed milk and bring to a boil,

The melting point of cocoa
butter is just below human
body temperature—this is why
chocolate melts in your mouth.

stirring constantly. Boil steadily for 5 to 10 minutes, until bubbles look like erupting volcanoes. Cook to 240°F or when a small amount of mixture forms a soft ball when dropped into a cup of cold water.

◆ Cool until bubbling stops.

◆ Beat well about 5 minutes, until mixture begins to thicken. This will give a smooth texture.

◆ Add chopped pecans and mix well.

◆ Pour into prepared baking pan and let stand 30 minutes, until half-set.

◆ Mark in 1-inch squares with a sharp knife and let stand until cold.

◆ Cut in squares, remove from baking pan, and store in candy jars or decorative boxes.

Torrone Molle
Makes 24 pieces

12 tablespoons unsalted butter, softened
6 oz. semisweet chocolate, melted, page 22
2/3 cup walnut halves, coarsely ground
1/3 cup blanched almonds, coarsely ground
1/3 cup hazelnuts, coarsely ground
1/2 cup sugar
3 tablespoons water
1 egg plus 1 yolk, beaten
1 tablespoon brandy
6 oz. petit beurre cookies

To Decorate:
Chocolate-coated blanched almonds, page 43

◆ Oil a jelly-roll pan.

◆ In a large bowl, beat butter and melted chocolate until smooth.

◆ Stir in all ground nuts.

◆ In a small saucepan, heat sugar and water until sugar is dissolved.

◆ Boil steadily until mixture reaches 240°F or until a small amount of mixture forms a soft ball when dropped into cold water.

◆ Cool a few minutes, then beat vigorously and pour into chocolate mixture, stirring until smooth.

◆ Stir in beaten egg and brandy.

◆ Break cookies in small, almond-size pieces. Stir gently into mixture.

◆ Turn into prepared pan and press to flatten. Cover and chill overnight.

◆ Remove from refrigerator just before serving and cut in diamond shapes.

◆ Decorate diamonds with chocolate-coated almonds.

Note: Instead of cutting in squares, torrone mixture may be spooned into a glass serving bowl and served as a firm, rich chocolate pudding.

Variation: Substitute 1²/₃ cups ground almonds for mixture of nuts to give a slightly different texture to the torrone.

▼ *Boil sugar and water in small saucepan.*

Praline & Sesame Sweets

Makes 20 to 24 pieces

¹/₂ cup sugar
³/₄ cup whole, unblanched almonds
1 tablespoon sesame seeds, toasted
2 oz. semisweet chocolate, melted, page 22

◆ Oil a baking sheet.

◆ In a small, heavy-bottomed saucepan, heat sugar and almonds very gently until sugar is dissolved.

◆ Cook gently until almonds begin to pop and turn brown and caramel is a rich brown color; shake pan so that almonds are coated with caramel.

◆ Pour in sesame seeds and shake pan to mix.

◆ Pour onto oiled baking sheet and let stand until hard.

◆ Break praline in large pieces and half-dip in

warm, melted chocolate. Shake off excess; place on waxed paper to set.

♦ Any broken pieces of praline can be coarsely chopped, mixed into remaining chocolate, and spooned in mounds on waxed paper.

Note: When exposed to a damp atmosphere, the praline may become rather sticky. To keep this from happening, coat completely with chocolate.

Variation: Replace almonds with hazelnuts and dip into chocolate to coat completely, if desired.

Chocolate-covered raisins, cherries, orange slices, and strawberries all count as fruit, so eat as many as you want!

Chocolate Fruit & Nuts

Makes 20 pieces

4 oz. semisweet chocolate, chopped
6 dates, pitted
8 dried apricots
¹/₂ cup slivered almonds

◆ In a small, heatproof bowl set over a pan of hot water, gently heat chocolate until melted.

◆ Using a skewer, dip each fruit into melted chocolate. Lift out and allow any excess chocolate to drip off.

◆ Place on waxed paper, carefully easing fruit off skewer with a second skewer. Let stand until chocolate has set.

◆ Toast almonds. Add to remaining chocolate and mix until well coated.

◆ Spoon onto waxed paper in six small circles and let stand until chocolate has set.

Note: Dates may be stuffed with almond paste.

Chocolate Marzipan Balls: Shape 4 oz. almond paste in cherry-sized balls and dip into melted chocolate to coat.

Chocolate Cherries: Divide 2 oz. almond paste in ten pieces and mold each piece around a glacé cherry to cover completely. Dip into melted chocolate to coat.

Chocolate Syrup
Makes 2 cups syrup

1 1/4 cups sugar
1 1/4 cups water
3/4 cup unsweetened cocoa powder

To Serve:
Milk
Vanilla ice cream
Whipped cream
Unsweetened cocoa powder, sifted

◆ In a small saucepan, heat sugar and water until sugar is dissolved.

◆ Bring to a boil; boil 3 minutes, stirring occasionally.

◆ Whisk in cocoa and continue whisking over moderate heat until smooth.

◆ Cool and refrigerate syrup until needed.

◆ For each serving, whisk 1 cup milk and 3 tablespoons chilled chocolate syrup.

◆ Pour into a chilled glass, add a scoop of ice cream, and top with whipped cream.

◆ Sprinkle with cocoa and serve immediately.

Note: This syrup can be refrigerated for several weeks and used as needed. It is an excellent topping for ice cream.

Hot Chocolate
Makes 1 or 2 servings

1¹/₂ oz. semisweet chocolate, chopped
1¹/₄ cups milk

◆ Place chocolate in a medium bowl.

◆ In a small saucepan, bring milk to a boil.

◆ Pour a fourth of the milk into the chocolate. Leave until chocolate has softened; whisk until smooth.

◆ Return remaining milk to the heat and bring back to a boil.

◆ Pour onto chocolate, whisking constantly.

◆ Serve immediately.

Variations:
Rum Toddy: Melt chocolate as above. Whisk in 2 tablespoons dark rum. Continue as above. Top with whipped cream and grated nutmeg.

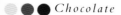

"Chocolate makes everyone smile—even bankers."
—Benneville Strohecker, Chocolatier

Spiced Chocolate: Add a good pinch each of grated nutmeg, ground allspice, and ground cinnamon to milk while heating in saucepan.

To serve, top with whipped cream and grated chocolate.

▼ *Alternatively stir chocolate into milk until dissolved.*

Hot Jucalette: Add 1 tablespoon sugar and
$1/4$ teaspoon ground cinnamon to milk while
heating in saucepan. Pour 1 tablespoon
whiskey into each heatproof glass; pour over
spiced milk. Top with whipped cream and fine
shreds of cinnamon stick.

Mocha: Dissolve 1 tablespoon instant coffee
granules in milk while heating. To serve, pour
1 tablespoon whipping cream over top of each
serving and sprinkle with chopped walnuts.

Chocolate Cocktails

Makes 1 serving each

Crème de Menthe Frappé

¹/₂ jigger crème de menthe
1 jigger crème de cacao
1 jigger whipping cream
Crushed ice

To serve:
Sprig of mint

◆ Place crème de menthe, crème de cacao, and whipping cream in a cocktail shaker and shake thoroughly.

◆ Half-fill a stemmed glass with crushed ice and pour cocktail over ice.

◆ Decorate with mint.

Variation: Use Cointreau instead of crème de menthe.

Rum Velvet

1 jigger dark crème de cacao
1 jigger dark rum
1 jigger whipping cream

To Finish:

Grated semisweet chocolate

◆ Pour crème de cacao and rum into a cocktail glass and stir to mix.

◆ Slowly and carefully pour whipping cream over back of a teaspoon into glass, so that it floats on top.

◆ Sprinkle with grated chocolate to serve.

Brandy Alexander

1 jigger crème de cacao
1 jigger brandy
1 jigger whipping cream
Crushed ice
Grated nutmeg

◆ Place crème de cacao, brandy, and whipping cream in a cocktail shaker.

◆ Add crushed ice and shake well.

◆ Strain into a cocktail glass and sprinkle with grated nutmeg to serve.

Almond & Chocolate Tuiles 343
Almond Curls 144
Almond Fingers 324, 336
Almond Fondue 68

Baking Chocolate 16
Banana–Chocolate Fudge Cake 265
Barcettos 303
Bombe aux Deux Chocolats 117
Bought Decorations 26
Brandy Alexander 395

Caraque, Chocolate 32
Carob 21
Chamonix 291
Chestnut & Orange Ice Cream 89
Chocolate & Brandy Bombe 113
Chocolate & Chestnut Cake 241
Chocolate & Pistachio Marquise 211

Chocolate-Chestnut Dessert 129
Chocolate-Chestnut Tart 199
Chocolate-Orange Cheesecake 207
Chocolate-Orange Cups 175
Chocolate-Vanilla Bombes 101
Chocolate-Strawberry Cones 181
Chocolate Almond Tartlets 307
Chocolate Brandy Creams 143
Chocolate Caramel Cake 225
Chocolate Checkerboards 329
Chocolate Cherries 385
Chocolate Christmas Pudding 155
Chocolate Cream Drops 299
Chocolate Fondue 67
Chocolate Fruit & Nuts 384
Chocolate Fudge Cake 261
Chocolate Japonais 283
Chocolate Marzipan Balls 385
Chocolate Meringue Nests 188

Chocolate Muffins 351
Chocolate Nut Fudge 373
Chocolate Pastry Tartlets 315
Chocolate Praline Cake 221
Chocolate Rondelles 279
Chocolate Roulade 253
Chocolate Soufflés 81
Chocolate Syrup 386
Chocolate Tagliatelle 63
Chocolate Terrine 167
Chocolate Truffle Cake 257
Chocolate Waffles 60
Chocolate Zabaglione 48
Chocolates, Homemade 40–41
Chocolatines 287
Clafoutis aux Cerises et Chocolat 75
Coating with Chocolate 43–45
Cocoa 19
Coeurs à la Crème au Chocolat 171

Cointreau Cream in Tulips 185
Collettes 369
Compound or Confectionery Coatings 18
Couverture 18
Cranberry & Pecan Cake 71
Cream Truffles 365
Crème de Menthe Frappé 393
Crème de Menthe Bombes 97
Cups, Chocolate 36–37
Curls, Chocolate 31

Decorations, Bought 26–29
Decorations, Homemade 30–37

Easter Eggs 39–40

Floretines 333
Frosted Mint Leaves 101
Frozen Chocolate-Orange Dessert 133

Frozen Mocha Soufflés 137
Frozen Praline Ring 109
Frozen Vanilla Slice 125

Ginger & Chocolate Meringues 295

Hazelnut Cake 273
Hazelnut-Chocolate Crescents 339
Hazelnut Galette with Kumquats 191
History of Chocolate, The 10–12
Horns, Chocolate 36
Hot Chocolate 389
Hot Jucalette 391

Introduction 8–9
Italian Baked Peaches 53

Leaves, Chocolate 32
Lebkuchen 355

Malibu Ice Cream 93
Marbled Chiffon Pie 215
Melting Chocolate 22–25
Milk Chocolate 17
Mocha 391
Mocha Chocolate Chip Cookies 348
Mocha Fondue 68
Molding Chocolate 38–42

Orange Fondue 69

Pains au Chocolat 319
Panforte di Siena 359
Pine Nut Fingers 325
Piped Chocolate 32–34
Pistachio Fingers 327
Praline & Sesame Sweets 381
Producing Chocolate 13–15
Profiteroles with Liqueur Cream 195

Ratafia Tortoni 121
Raspberry-Chocolate Brûlées 163
Rich Chocolate Ice Cream 86
Rich Mocha Cake 269
Rum Fudge Pudding 78
Rum & Raisin Cheesecake 203
Rum Toddy 389
Rum Velvet 394

Sacher Torte 233
Semisweet Chocolate 16
Shapes, Chocolate 34–36
Shells, Chocolate 37
Sicilian Cassata 247
Speckled Ice Cream 105
Spiced Chocolate 390
St. Emilion Dessert 147
Steamed Chocolate Pudding 159
Storing Chocolate 20

Striped Chocolate Cake 249
Strawberry-Chocolate Crepes 57
Strawberry-Chocolate Tarts 311
Strawberry Cake 229
Sweets, Homemade Chocolate & 40–41

Torrone Molle 377
Types of Chocolate 16–18

Walnut & Chocolate Fingers 323
White Chocolate 17
White Chocolate Mousse 177

Yule Log 237

Zuccotto 151